ROBERT FULGHUM'S

ALL I REALLY NEED TO KNOW
I LEARNED IN KINDERGARTEN

Conceived and Adapted by
ERNEST ZULIA

Music and Lyrics by
DAVID CALDWELL

[Handwritten annotations:]

Act I
Yes, OF course I can!
Cinderella!
Larry Walters Flies!
Bransley Spider!
~~Beeth~~ Beethoven!
(opt) Donnie!
Stuff in the Sink!
The Bench! ✈

Act II
MOTB!
Pidgeons!
Breifcase!
Geek Dancing!
Tomb w/ a Veiw!
Any Questions?!

Prob. & Intro.
Ed.
Breifcase - Ed

Dramatic Publishing
Woodstock, Illinois • London, England • Melbourne, Australia

*** NOTICE ***

©MCMXCIX
Script created and adapted by
ERNEST ZULIA
Music, lyrics, musical arrangements, and orchestration by
DAVID CALDWELL
Based upon the essays by
ROBERT FULGHUM

Printed in the United States of America
All Rights Reserved
(ALL I REALLY NEED TO KNOW I LEARNED IN KINDERGARTEN)

ISBN 0-87129-913-5

IMPORTANT BILLING AND CREDIT REQUIREMENTS

Check out the *Kindergarten* website for:

- the most recent discoveries and insights on ways of presenting *All I Really Need to Know I Learned in Kindergarten*, including authorized script and score changes, effective staging devices, and alternate story and song sequences.

- information on recordings of songs, sound effects and piano accompaniment for rehearsal and performance.

- information on the sequel, *Uh-Oh, Here Comes Christmas*.

allireallyneed.com.

The following notice and list of books should appear on the title page or in another prominent location in the playbill.

"This production includes material from Robert Fulghum's books:"

All I Really Need to Know I Learned in Kindergarten
It Was on Fire When I Lay Down on It
Uh-Oh
Maybe, Maybe Not
From Beginning to End

* * * *

Acknowledgments

For all their help and support, many thanks go to: John Corker, Barbara Witt, Dr. Susan Dornacker, Jere Hodgin, Jo Weinstein, David Zoffoli, John Sloman, and the many actors, directors, designers and producers who have contributed so much to the development of this show.

Contents

(The following is the sequence for the full-musical version of the show. Please see Production Notes in the appendix for sequence adjustments for the reduced-musical version.)

The original production of *All I Really Need to Know I Learned in Kindergarten* premiered in July 1992 at Mill Mountain Theatre, Roanoke, Va. It was directed by Ernest Zulia, designed by John Sailer, and featured the following cast:

Kathleen .... KATHLEEN BUTLER
Jill .... JILL JANE CLEMENTS
Ed .... ED SALA
Branislav .... BRANISLAV TOMICH
Fred .... FREDERICK WALTERS
Narrator/Stage Manager .... RACHEL HOHN
Pianist/Singer .... DAVID CALDWELL

The play was later produced at Ford's Theatre in Washington D.C., directed by Ernest Zulia, with the following cast:

Jill .... BONNIE FRANKLIN
Ed .... GARY HOLCOMBE
Kathleen .... LIZ SHERIDAN
Branislav .... LARA TEETER
Fred .... JAMES WHITMORE
Narrator/Conductor .... DAVID CALDWELL

Author's Notes

About the Script

This stage adaptation is primarily a storytelling piece which is intended to be performed with simplicity, honesty, and humor. It is comprised of stories from Robert Fulghum's first five best-selling books, which sold over 15 million copies in 93 countries, and have been translated into 27 languages. These entertaining stories are primarily about ordinary people. The author's comic style delivers an insightful and heartfelt perspective on everyday life, and the profound echoes that reverberate through it.

The show, as presented in this published script, has been developed in front of a variety of audiences, in the United States and abroad, and is felt to be the optimal way to perform *Kindergarten.* However, it can be adjusted to suit specific situations and audiences. It can be presented as a full musical (with seven songs), or in a "reduced-musical" version (which is more like a play with music, and has also been referred to as the "non-musical version." See Appendix A for details.) The show can be shortened or lengthened; the cast can be expanded; and some stories, lines, or songs can be reassigned. There are author's notes in the appendix that will assist in some of these choices, and there is a section devoted to a special high-school version of the script. There is a full piano/vocal score under separate cover with cues and notes for all versions. In spite of all the variations and options offered throughout this script, the show as presented in the table of contents ("full musical" or "reduced musical"), and executed by a five-person cast, is considered the most effective way to present *All I Really Need to Know I Learned in Kindergarten.*

About the Cast

The five actors should have strong comedic and dramatic skills, as well as natural storytelling ability. A variety of different personalties within the cast can be valuable. A generosity of spirit helps communicate the essence of the material, and keen wit keeps them from becoming patronizing, pious, or cloying. They present the stories as if they were occurrences out of their own lives.

In the musical version of the show, the sung material assigned to Branislav, Jill, and Ed requires strong singing voices; the material covered by Kathleen and Fred is less demanding. For the non-musical version, at least one fairly strong singer (an actor, the narrator, or the pianist) is required to cover the title song, and possibly "Reflect the Light."

The character names listed on the following page and throughout the script are those of the actors who created the roles in the original workshop. It is expected that each production will utilize the names of its own cast members in the script and in the playbill.

The ages of these characters are appropriate to the material assigned to each, and the age range is extremely valuable to the resonance of the material. However, in certain situations, age ranges could be adjusted, and/or the size of the cast could be expanded.

ALL I REALLY NEED TO KNOW I LEARNED IN KINDERGARTEN

A Comedy
For 3 Men, 2 Women, 1 pianist
(may be expanded—ages somewhat flexible)

CHARACTERS

FRED. . . . . late 50s to late 60s

ED . . . . late 40s to early 50s

BRANISLAV . . . . mid-30s to 40

JILL. . . . . mid-30s to early 40s

KATHLEEN . . . . late 50s to 60s

NARRATOR. . . . . a voice over the sound system
(Can also be performed by a separate actor or by the
pianist/singer.)

DAVID . . (optional onstage character) pianist/singer (m or f)
(Can also function as Narrator. In the reduced-musical
version, this character can play and sing the title song.)

Note: See p. 112 in Appendix A for more in-depth character descriptions.

ACT ONE

(Lights go to black—PIANO TRANSITION.)

YES! OF COURSE I CAN!

(Lights come up on the five actors seated in plain wooden school chairs facing the audience. They are kindergartners but remain very quiet and still until the first explosion of enthusiasm after the narrator's first line. There is a free-standing chalkboard behind them with a large question mark drawn on it. The narrator is heard over the sound system and never seen. If the pianist serves as narrator, a microphone should still be used, giving the same effect of a disembodied voice. Even though the audience may be able to see him/her, the actors should not acknowledge his/her physical presence. The actors start as enthusiastic five-year-olds, then transform into cautiously "cool" college students and finally into reticent adults. Their focus is on an imaginary person out front.)

NARRATOR. Ask a kindergarten class, "How many of you can draw?" and all hands shoot up.

ALL *(actors as kindergartners vocalize with tremendous enthusiasm as their hands shoot up indicating "pick me." A variation of this gesture is repeated every time the word "Yes!" is spoken throughout the show).* Oooo Oooo Oooo Oooo Oooo!

1

FRED (*as kindergartner speaking above the others*). Oooo Ooo Ooo Ooo Ooo! ... Yes, of course we can draw!

KATHLEEN. All of us!

NARRATOR. What can you draw?

ED. Anything!

NARRATOR. How about a dog eating a fire truck in the jungle?

BRANISLAV. Sure! How big do you want it?!

NARRATOR. How many of you can sing?

ALL (*again an enthusiastic vocal and physical reaction*). Oooo Oooo Oooo!

JILL (*speaking above the others*). Yes! Of course we can sing!

NARRATOR. What can you sing?

KATHLEEN. Anything!

NARRATOR. What if you don't know the words?

JILL. That's OK! We'll make them up.

BRANISLAV & JILL. Let's sing!

NARRATOR. Now?

BRANISLAV. Why not? (*They each improvise a song.*)

NARRATOR. How many of you dance?

ALL (*hands shoot up with the same vocal and physical enthusiasm*). Ooo Ooo Ooo Ooo!

NARRATOR. What kind of music do you like to dance to?

ED. Any kind. Let's dance!

NARRATOR. Now?

ED. Sure, why not? (*Spontaneously does a brief improvised dance.*)

NARRATOR. Do you like to act in plays?

ALL (*hands shoot up. BRANISLAV and JILL rise and remain up*). Yes!

NARRATOR. Do you play musical instruments?

ALL (*hands shoot up. ED rises, remains up*). Yes!

NARRATOR. Do you write poetry?

ALL (*hands shoot up. KATHLEEN rises, remains up*). Yes!

NARRATOR. Can you read and write and count?

ALL (*hands shoot up*). Yes!

FRED (*rising with great enthusiasm and pride*). We're learning that stuff now.

NARRATOR. Try those same questions on a college audience. (*Short PIANO TRANSITION.*)

(*There is a moment of panic as the college students realize how "uncool" they must look with hands in the air and enthusiastic body postures. As inconspicuously as possible, their hands come down, and they sit, assuming the posture and attitude of self-conscious college students trying to be cool.*)

NARRATOR (*after transition is complete*). A few students will raise their hands when asked if they can draw or dance or sing or paint or act or play an instrument. More often than not, those who do raise their hands will want to qualify their responses with their limitations.

BRANISLAV. I play piano—but not very well—my mother made me.

ED. I only dance to rock and roll.

JILL. I only sing in the shower.

FRED (*topping the others with a wisecrack*). I only draw conclusions. (*All laugh with audience.*)

NARRATOR. When asked why the limitations, college students answer:

KATHLEEN. I don't have any talent.

ED. I haven't done any of that stuff since about the third grade.

FRED. Who's got the time?

BRANISLAV. That's not my major.

NARRATOR. You can imagine the response to the same question asked of an older audience. *(Short PIANO TRAN-SITION.)*

(There is a stunned moment of silence while they all transform to adults. Each is mortified that they will be asked to dance or sing or act. After the moment sinks in, all attempt to escape, ad-libbing, but <u>clearly heard by the audience</u> as they cross U.)

ALL *(ad-libbing).* "Oh gee. Is that the time?" "Gotta run," "I don't think so," "You've got to be kidding," "Maybe after about three martinis," etc. *(All freeze U. PIANO INTRO begins for "The Kindergarten Song.")*

NARRATOR. What went wrong between kindergarten and now? Whatever happened to "Yes! Of course I can"? *(SOUND CUE: School bell rings.)*

"THE KINDERGARTEN SONG"

JILL.

(VERSE 1)

    I'VE BECOME SO CAUGHT UP IN MY
       GROWN-UP STUFF
    IT SEEMS I'VE LOST MY SPONTANEITY,
    NOT TO MENTION PERSPECTIVE ON LIVING
       LIFE,

**EVERY DAY, AT MY JOB, WITH MY FAMILY.
BUT I'M DISCOVERING**

ALL.

**ALL I REALLY NEED TO KNOW I LEARNED IN
KINDERGARTEN,**

ED.

ABOUT HOW TO LIVE,

FRED.

WHAT TO DO,

BRANISLAV.

HOW TO BE.

JILL.

**IT'S THE SANDBOX CODE OF ETHICS, NOT
SOME GRAD SCHOOL MUMBO-JUMBO
THAT'S HAD THE GREATEST IMPACT ON ME.**

*(KATHLEEN flips the chalkboard to reveal the Kinder-
garten Creed. See Appendix F for exact text.)*

(CHORUS)

JILL.

I LEARNED: SHARE.

KATHLEEN.

PLAY FAIR.

FRED.
>   **DON'T HIT PEOPLE.**

ED.
>   **DON'T TAKE THINGS THAT DON'T BELONG TO
>   YOU.**

BRANISLAV.
>   **IF YOU HURT SOMEONE, SAY YOU'RE SORRY—**

JILL.
>   **TO NAME JUST A FEW.
>   CLEAN UP YOUR OWN MESS,**

KATHLEEN.
>   **AND WASH YOUR HANDS BEFORE YOU EAT.**

ALL.
>   **HOLD HANDS AND STICK TOGETHER WHEN
>   YOU CROSS THE STREET.**

BRANISLAV.
>   **FLUSH.**

ED.
>   **LIVE A BALANCED LIFE—LEARN SOME, THINK
>   SOME, WORK AND PLAY,**

BRANISLAV.
>   **AND SING AND DANCE AND DRAW,**

FRED.
>   **AND TAKE A NAP EACH DAY.**

ALL.

> BE AWARE OF WONDER.

KATHLEEN.

> THINK OF THE SEED IN THE PAPER CUP—
> WHO KNOWS WHY THE ROOT GOES DOWN
>   AND THE PLANT GOES UP?
> BUT WE'RE ALL LIKE THAT;
> AND JUST AS THE SEED, THE
> MOUSE, THE BEE,
> AND THE GOLDFISH, WILL ALL
> DIE SOME DAY, WELL, SO WILL WE.

ALL.

> REMEMBER THE FIRST WORD YOU LEARNED
>   IN YOUR DICK-AND-JANE BOOK—
> THE BIGGEST, MOST IMPORTANT WORD OF ALL:
> LOOK ...

BRANISLAV *(referring to the written Creed).*

> *(VERSE 2)*
> EVERYTHING YOU NEED TO KNOW IS IN
>   THERE SOMEWHERE,
> FROM THE GOLDEN RULE TO BASIC
>   SANITATION.
> REALLY I HAVE KNOWN THESE THINGS ALL
>   MY LIFE.
> LIVING THEM—WELL, THAT'S ANOTHER
>   CONVERSATION.

ED.

> APPLY ANY OF THESE ITEMS TO YOUR
>   GOVERNMENT,

YOUR WORLD, YOUR FAMILY LIFE OR YOUR
    CAREER;
TRANSLATE THEM INTO SOPHISTICATED
    GROWN-UP TERMS,
AND THEY WILL ALL HOLD TRUE AND FIRM
    AND CLEAR.

FRED.
  (VERSE 3)
    IF WE ALL STOPPED TO TAKE A NAP EACH DAY,
    THINK HOW MUCH BETTER OUR WORLD
        WOULD BE.
    AND WHAT IF CLEANING UP THEIR OWN MESS
    WERE A MATTER OF OUR GOVERNMENT'S
        POLICY?

ALL.
    AND IT'S STILL TRUE, WHEN WE GO OUT INTO
        THE WORLD
    IN THESE UNCERTAIN TIMES, UNCERTAIN
        WEATHER—
    IT DOESN'T MATTER IF YOU'RE SIX YEARS
        OLD OR SIXTY—
    WE SHOULD ALL HOLD HANDS AND STICK
        TOGETHER.

    REMEMBER THE FIRST WORD YOU LEARNED
        IN YOUR DICK-AND-JANE BOOK—
    THE BIGGEST MOST IMPORTANT WORD OF ALL:

    LOOK...

*(The actors form a line across the stage as KATHLEEN
passes out four placards, careful not to reveal what is*

printed on one side. Just as they begin to sing the word
LOOK, the actors lift the placards over their heads, re-
vealing the letters that should have spelled the word
"LOOK," but they were scrambled up and spelled
"OLOK." They catch their mistake just before they at-
tempt to sing the word LOOK. They scramble around, ar-
rive at new positions, and once again they start to sing
the word LOOK, only to discover that they have now
spelled "LOKO." One more scramble, and they are fi-
nally in the correct positions, spelling the word "LOOK,"
which they now finally sing. On the last note of the mu-
sic, just before the cut-off, the two "O"'s make one final
switch, as though it made a difference which "O" is
right or left. The fifth actor [KATHLEEN] serves as di-
rector of this whole fiasco, and joins in the final picture
with a placard revealing an exclamation point. Note:
The above antics are set to specific music cues which
are noted in the score.)

CINDERELLA

(JILL erases question mark, and writes "CINDERELLA"
on chalkboard.)

ED. Cinderella was the title on the chalkboard marquee.

FRED. Given the task of dramatizing a fairy tale for a
teacher's conference, the kindergarten class decided on
the classic old rags-to-riches story, "Cinderella."

BRANISLAV. You know how it goes: "Shy agreeable pro-
tagonist, victimized by abusive step-parent, waits for

wise matriarchal figure to rescue her, and deliver her transformed from co-dependency to bliss."

KATHLEEN. In other words; if you're good-looking, good at heart, and have a fairy godmother ... you got it made.

JILL. It was a good choice from the teacher's point of view, because there were so many characters and every child in the class could be in the play.

ED. A list of characters was compiled as the class talked through the plot of the drama.

KATHLEEN. There was the absolutely ravishing Cinderella,

FRED. the evil stepmother,

ED & BRANISLAV. the two wicked but stupid stepsisters,

JILL. the beautiful and wise fairy godmother,

BRANISLAV. the pumpkin,

ED. mice,

KATHLEEN. coachmen,

FRED. horses,

BRANISLAV. king,

JILL. all the people at the King's ball,

ED. generals,

FRED. admirals,

BRANISLAV. knights,

KATHLEEN. princesses,

ED. and, of course, that ultimate object of fabled desire *(Strikes a cocky pose.)* ... the Prince.

FRED *(referring to ED)*. Who, if you recall, was really only a salesman interested in pushing his inventory of glass slippers.

JILL. The children were allowed to choose roles for themselves. As the parts were allotted, each child was labeled with felt pen and paper, and sent to stand over on the other side of the room while casting was completed. Finally, every child had a part.

FRED *(could also be spoken by an actor not playing Norman).* Except one. One small boy. Who had remained quiet and disengaged from the selection process. Norman. A kid who was somehow different—not weird, just different—in the way he looked at things. Norman was always thinking. And like so many misunderstood, but great thinkers, Norman was teased a lot by his classmates, causing him to live on the fringe of kindergarten society. *(He has transformed himself into Norman—a deeply earnest and serious individual.)*

JILL *(as the teacher).* "Well, Norman," said the teacher, "what are you going to be?"

FRED. "Well, I am going to be the pig."

JILL. "Pig? There is no pig in the story of Cinderella."

FRED *(after a long pause, matter-of-factly).* "Well... There is now."

BRANISLAV. Norman did not relate to being a footman or a mouse or a pumpkin.

ED. He knew his character. Pig.

KATHLEEN. And he was not about to give up his part in the play and go over and stand against the wall where a loser would stand.

ED. He intended to participate wherever pigs fit into the scheme of things. Without giving up dignity or identity. He took it for granted that there was a place for pigs, and that the teacher would know that.

BRANISLAV. So what do you say to a kid who is already thinking up a costume of pink long underwear, pipe-cleaner tail, and a paper cup for a nose?

ED. What do you say to an innocent little pig who doesn't see his career as an actor teetering on the brink of utter humiliation?

KATHLEEN *(to audience, knowing this is the real question)*. And what do you say to all the pigs? All those who are different and who do not accept the available boxes and pigeonholes?

ED. So, what did the teacher say at the moment...?

BRANISLAV *(looking at JILL, who is thinking very hard about how to handle this delicate situation)*. Well, sometimes teachers talk more like fairy godmothers.

JILL *(after a pause, a flourish from the PIANO suggesting the waving of a magic wand)*. So be it!

FRED. Norman was declared the pig in the story of Cinderella.

JILL. It was quite fine with the rest of the class; nobody else wanted to be the pig anyhow.

ED. And since there was nothing in the script explaining what the pig was supposed to do, the action was left up to Norman. As it turned out, Norman gave himself one of the all-time best walk-on parts in the history of children's theater. He decided he was Cinderella's "personal pig." *(Pause.)* Where she went...he went. *(Pause.)*

BRANISLAV. He made no sound. *(Norman acts out the following narration.)* He simply sat on his back haunches and observed what was going on, like some silently supportive Greek chorus.

KATHLEEN. The expressions on his face reflected the details of the dramatic action. Looking worried, *(Norman responds with intense, earnest facial expressions for each emotion. He is focused and genuinely engaged in the drama of the story.)*

ED. sad,

BRANISLAV. anxious,

KATHLEEN. hopeful,

BRANISLAV. puzzled,

ED. mad,

KATHLEEN. bored,

BRANISLAV. sick,

ED. and pleased... as the moment required.

BRANISLAV. There was no doubt about what was going on, and no doubt that it was important.

KATHLEEN. One look at the pig and you knew. The pig was so earnest. So sincere. So very... "there."

ED. Norman created such dramatic tension that people who knew how this story was supposed to end... began to have doubts.

BRANISLAV. At the climax, when the Prince finally placed the glass slipper on Cinderella's foot and the ecstatic couple hugged and rode off to live happily ever after, Norman *finally* made his move. *(Norman explodes into a spontaneous dance of joy with reckless abandon.)* He went wild with joy, dancing around the stage on his back feet... *("Norman" barks wildly, ending with a long howl.. <u>When he stops</u>, BRANISLAV takes a beat, then finishes his line.)* ...and barking like a dog.

JILL. In rehearsal, the teacher had tried explaining to Norman: "Even if there was a pig in the Cinderella story, there is no such thing as a dancing, barking pig."

FRED *(long pause; matter-of-factly).* "Well, there is now." *(He stands there holding his ground as the teacher contemplates this statement.)*

JILL *(considers Norman with solemn respect, realizing there is an undeniability about Norman's position).* It's true Norman, it's true... Knock 'em dead, pig! *(PIANO MUSIC: Magic wand flourish.)*

BRANISLAV. The presentation at the teachers' conference was a smash hit! *(Lights shift, Norman repeats his dance in slow motion.)*

KATHLEEN *(with a sense of profound appreciation for the miraculous transformation that is taking place)*. When Norman danced his dance, the crowd of weary teachers laughed... and wept... and cheered.

BRANISLAV. And later, when the pig stumbled out for his curtain call, the applause turned into a spontaneous standing ovation. *(Norman crosses DC for his bow. SOUND CUE: Thunderous applause and cheering.)*

KATHLEEN *(sound cue fades)*. The teachers were able to see that the *real* Cinderella was not the little girl with the button nose and blonde hair... but Norman, the dancing, barking pig.

ED. And they knew the real fairy godmother was not the child waving her fairy wand, but the teacher, standing, weeping in the wings.

KATHLEEN. Kindergarten teachers know magic when they see it. *(PIANO FLOURISH: Magic wand cue.)*

BRANISLAV *(as an epilogue)*. Well, the kindergarten class had many invitations to come and perform their highly acclaimed production of "Cinderella." Sometimes the teacher would have to explain what it was about the performance that was so unique.

JILL. "It has a pig in it, you see?"

ED. "Oh, really?"

JILL. "Yes, the star of the show is... a dancing, barking pig."

ED. "But there is no dancing, barking pig in 'Cinderella.' "

JILL, BRANISLAV, FRED, KATHLEEN. Well. There is now!

(PIANO TRANSITION: Lights bump to transition. PIANO continues under SOUND CUE.)

HIDE AND SEEK

(SOUND CUE: Children laughing and playing. ED, as a child, runs on and hides under the window but is fully visible to the audience. He is unaware of KATHLEEN.)

KATHLEEN *(with a mix of nostalgia and droll wit, referring to ED).* In the early dry dark of an October's evening, the neighborhood children are playing hide-and-seek. How long since I played hide-and-seek. Forty years? *(Sensing doubt from the audience.)* OK, maybe more. I remember how and I could join in their game in a moment, if they invited me. But adults don't play hide-and-seek. Not for fun, anyway.

(Not referring to ED.) Did you have a kid in your neighborhood who always hid "so good," nobody could find him? We did. After a while we would give up on him and go off, leaving him to *rot* wherever he was. Sooner or later he would show up, all mad because we didn't keep looking for him. And we would get mad back because he wasn't playing the game the way it was supposed to be played. There's HIDING and there's FINDING, we'd say. And he'd say it was "hide-and-seek, not hide-and-give-UP," and we'd all yell about who made the rules and who cared about who, anyway, and how

we wouldn't play with him anymore if he didn't get it straight, and things like that. Hide-and-seek...and-yell. No matter what, though, the next time he would hide too good again. He's probably still hiding somewhere, for all I know.

This neighborhood game goes on, *(Crosses to window and indicates ED hiding.)* and there is a kid under my front window, hiding in a pile of leaves. He has been there for some time now, and everybody else is found and they are about to give up on him over at the base. I considered going out to the base and telling them where he is hiding. And I thought about setting the leaves on fire. Finally, I just yelled, "GET FOUND, KID!" *(ED is startled, reacts, runs offstage crying.)* It's hard to know how to be helpful sometimes.

(With an air of compassionate insight, rather than grief or judgment.) A man I know found out last year he had terminal cancer. He was a doctor. And knew about dying, and he didn't want to make his family and friends suffer through that with him. So he kept his secret. And he died. Everybody said how brave he was to bear his suffering in silence. But privately his family and friends said how angry they were that he didn't need them, didn't trust their strength. And they were hurt that he hadn't said goodbye. He hid "too good." Getting found would have kept him in the game.

Hide-and-seek, grown-up style. Wanting to hide. Needing to be sought. Confused about being found.

Better than hide-and-seek, I like a game called "sardines"!

(PIANO MUSIC: BRANISLAV enters looking for a place to hide.)

Now in sardines, the person who is "it" goes and hides. *(BRANISLAV hides.)* And everybody goes looking for him.

(ED enters—looks for BRANISLAV and spots him.)

But, when they find him, they don't let anybody know; *(ED hides with BRANISLAV.)* ...instead they get in and hide there with him.

(As the next line is being spoken, JILL runs on looking for the others, finds them and jumps on the pile.)

Pretty soon everybody is hiding together, all stacked in a heap like a pile of puppies.
(They shush each other and sit in a moment of silent anticipation.)
　　And then somebody giggles
(JILL giggles, FRED shushes her. Silence.)
　　...then somebody laughs
(Unable to hold it back, one bursts out laughing. The others can't help joining in, and it escalates. KATHLEEN sneaks up on the heap and shouts, startling them.)
　　...and everybody GETS FOUND!!!
(Caught by KATHLEEN who is the last player, they all jump up and run off laughing hysterically, leaving KATHLEEN alone onstage. Drawing the parallel between the adults and children, she says:)
　　By the sound of laughter, everybody gets found.

(PIANO TRANSITION. KATHLEEN drops all adult dignity and as the lights fade, she runs off trying to catch

up with the children to join in their game. Note: from this point forward, the show ceases to deal directly with kindergarten.)

LARRY WALTERS FLIES

(FRED, as Larry Walters, enters with old-fashioned aluminum chaise lounge lawn chair, with fiberglass webbing. He finds the "sunniest" spot, unfolds the chair and sits. JILL, ED and BRANISLAV enter looking on.)

JILL. True story.

BRANISLAV. True story.

ED. True story. Larry Walters.

ED, BRANISLAV, JILL. Our hero.

BRANISLAV. Walters is a truck driver. Your average guy. He is sitting in his lawn chair in his backyard, wishing he could fly.

JILL. For as long as he could remember, he wanted to go UP. To be high up in the air somehow—to ride the sky.

ED. But there was no way he was ever going to pilot a plane—and hang-gliding just looked too dangerous.

JILL. So he spent a lot of summer afternoons sitting in his backyard in his ordinary old aluminum lawn chair—the kind with the webbing and rivets.

(PIANO MUSIC. Stage fills with cloud gobos. Window unit flies out. The narrators are amazed and delighted by Larry's unbelievable outrageousness.)

BRANISLAV. The next chapter takes place on July 2, 1982, and appears on television and in newspapers across the country.

ED. There's old Larry Walters up in the air over Los Angeles. Flying at last.

JILL. Really getting up there.

BRANISLAV. Still sitting in his aluminum lawn chair. Only *now* it's hooked up to forty-five helium-filled surplus weather balloons.

ED. Larry has a parachute on, a CB radio, a six-pack of ~~beer~~ drinks, some peanut butter and jelly sandwiches, and a BB gun to pop some of the balloons to come down.

JILL. But instead of being just a couple of hundred feet over his neighborhood, he SHOT UP ELEVEN THOUSAND FEET, RIGHT THROUGH THE APPROACH CORRIDOR TO THE LOS ANGELES INTERNATIONAL AIRPORT. *(SOUND CUE: Jet plane sweeping by with a roar. Larry reacts to his near collision with the jet.)* This is a true story.

ED. The human race sits in its chair, some saying there's nothing left to do,

BRANISLAV. ...others that the human situation is hopeless.

JILL. Meanwhile, the Larry Walters of the world are busy tying balloons to their chairs.

BRANISLAV. When asked by the press why he did it, he said:

FRED. "You can't just sit there."

JILL. When asked if he was scared, he answered:

FRED *(delighted)*. "You bet."

ED. When asked if he would do it again, he said:

FRED *(without hesitation)*. "Nope."

JILL. When asked: "Are you glad you did it?"

BRANISLAV. "Are you glad you did it?"

ED. "Are you glad you did it?"

JILL. He grinned from ear to ear and said:

FRED *(to JILL)*. "Yes." *(To BRANISLAV.)* "Yes." *(To ED.)* "Yes!" *(He exits with chair. Shouting from the wings.)* Oh YES!!!

BRANISLAV. If the dream is held close to the heart...

ED. And imagination is applied to what there is close at hand...

JILL. Everything is still possible.

(PIANO TRANSITION. Lights fade.)

"CHARLES BOYER"
(The Song)

(PIANO segues into a French waltz. ED enters with a stool.)

ED. This is kind of personal. It started as a note to my wife. And then I thought that since some of you might feel the same way, I'd pass it along. I don't own this story, anyway. Charles Boyer does. *(Slide of Charles Boyer appears on back wall.)*
  REMEMBER CHARLES BOYER?
  SUAVE, DAPPER, HANDSOME, KING OF THE
    MATINEE,
  LOVER OF THE FAIREST WOMEN OF THE
    SILVER SCREEN,
  AS YOU COULD READ IN ANY FAN MAGAZINE.
(He sits.)

> BUT IN REAL LIFE,
> THERE WAS ONLY ONE WOMAN: PATRICIA,
>   HIS WIFE.
> THEY SHARED A LIFETIME OF LAUGHTER
>   AND TEARS;
> THEY WERE FRIENDS, COMPANIONS AND
>   LOVERS FOR FORTY-FOUR YEARS.

Then Patricia developed cancer of the liver. And so he stayed by her side to provide hope and cheer. Day and night for six months. But he could not change the inevitable. And Patricia died in his arms. Two days later Charles Boyer was also dead. By his own hand. He said that he did not want to live without her. He said, "Her love was life." This was no movie. As I say, it's the real story—Charles Boyer's story.

It's not for me to judge how he handled his grief. But it is for me to say that I am *touched* and *comforted* in a strange way. *Touched* by the depth of love behind the apparent sham of Hollywood love life. *Comforted* to know that two people can love each other that much that long. I don't know how I would handle my grief in similar circumstances. I pray I shall never have to stand in his shoes. *(Slide fades away.)* Here comes the personal part—no apologies. *(He rises, sings.)*

> BUT NOWADAYS,
> THERE ARE TIMES WHEN I STOP TO GAZE

(Focuses toward imagined image of his wife.)

> AT MY FRIEND, COMPANION AND WIFE,
> AMID THE ROUTINE OF DAILY LIFE,

(Focuses to audience, or Boyer.)

> AND SOMEHOW I KNOW
> HOW BOYER MUST HAVE FELT YEARS AGO.

(Focuses back to image of his imagined wife.)
**SHE STILL MOVES ME— HER VOICE, HER
    TOUCH—
IT REALLY IS POSSIBLE
TO LOVE SOMEONE *THAT MUCH*.**

(PIANO MUSIC continues into TRANSITION, as ED exits.)

CHARLES BOYER
(Alternate spoken version)

*(PIANO MUSIC segues into a French waltz. ED enters
with a stool.)*

ED. This is kind of personal. It started as a note to my
wife. And then I thought that since some of you might
feel the same way, I'd pass it along. I don't own this
story, anyway. Charles Boyer does. *(Slide of Charles
Boyer appears on back wall.)*

Remember Charles Boyer? Suave, dapper, handsome,
graceful. Lover of the most famous and beautiful women
of the silver screen. That was on camera and in the fan
magazines. *(He sits.)*

In real life it was different. There was only one
woman. For forty-four years. His wife, Patricia. Friends
said it was a lifelong love affair. They were no less lovers and friends and companions after forty-four years
than after the first year.

Then Patricia developed cancer of the liver. And so
he stayed by her side to provide hope and cheer. Day
and night for six months. But he could not change the

inevitable. And Patricia died in his arms. Two days later Charles Boyer was also dead. By his own hand. He said that he did not want to live without her. He said, "Her love was life."

This was no movie. As I say, it's the real story—Charles Boyer's story.

It's not for me to judge how he handled his grief. But it is for me to say that I am *touched* and *comforted* in a strange way. *Touched* by the depth of love behind the apparent sham of Hollywood love life. *Comforted* to know that two people can love each other that much, that long.

I don't know how I would handle my grief in similar circumstances. I pray I shall never have to stand in his shoes. *(Slide fades away, ED rises. PIANO MUSIC.)*

Here comes the personal part—no apologies.

There are moments when I look across the room—amid the daily ordinariness of life—and see the person I call my wife and friend and companion. And, although I may not understand why Charles Boyer did what he did—I know how he felt. It really is possible to love someone *that much*. I know. I'm absolutely certain of it.

(PIANO TRANSITION.)

BEETHOVEN

(SOUND CUE: Phone ringing interrupts the MUSIC TRANSITION and/or breaks the applause. BRANISLAV enters talking on a mimed cordless phone.)

BRANISLAV *(holding the phone to his chest, speaks to the audience).* Talking with a friend on the phone. She has a case of the mid-winter spiritual rot. And a terminal cold she's had since September.

JILL *(onstage, or over the microphone).* Well, you don't ever get depressed, do you?

BRANISLAV *(into the phone).* Are you kidding? There are times when I get so low it takes an extension ladder to climb out.

JILL. So what do you do? I mean, WHAT DO YOU DO?

BRANISLAV *(JILL exits, phone disappears. To audience).* No one ever pinned me down quite like that before. They usually ask what I think *they* should do.

My solace is not religion or yoga or rum or even deep sleep. *(Pause.)* It's...Beethoven. I put his Ninth Symphony on the stereo, pull the earphones down tight, and lie down on the floor. *(He lies down on floor in a pool of light, or at least suggests this activity.)*

(Listening through the imaginary earphones, clearly moved by what he hears.) The music comes on like the first day of Creation.

And I think about old Mr. B. *(He sits up, removing his earphones, and speaks casually to the audience.)* He knew a whole lot about depression and unhappiness. He moved around from place to place trying to find the right place. Had a lousy love life. Quarreled with his friends all the time. Mr. B. wanted to be a virtuoso pianist. He wanted to sing well, too. But when he was still quite young, he began to lose his hearing. Which is usually bad news for pianists and singers. By 1818, when he was forty-eight, he was stone-cold deaf. Which makes it all the more *amazing* that he completed his great Ninth Symphony five years later.

He never really heard it.

(Truly amazed.) He just *thought* it!

So I lie there with my earphones on, wondering if it could ever have felt to Beethoven the way it sounds in my head. *(SOUND CUE: The last 30 seconds of the final movement of the Ninth. Actually begins on the word "...wondering," and achieves audibility by the word "...head." [See note on p. 26-27.] BRANISLAV rises as he speaks and passionately demonstrates his outrageous living-room performance in all its joy, exuberance and ridiculousness.)* The crescendo rises, and my sternum starts to vibrate. And by the time the final kettledrum drowns out all those big chords, I'm on my feet, singing along in gibberish German with the mighty choir, and jumping up and down during the final awesome moments of the END OF THE WORLD AND THE COMING OF GOD AND ALL HIS ANGELS, HALLELUJAH! HALLELUJAH! WWHOOOOOOO-OOMM-KABOOM-BANG!! LORD!!

Uplifted! exalted! excited! affirmed! and overwhelmed! MANALIVE! Out of all that sorrow and trouble, out of all that frustration and disappointment, out of all that deep and permanent silence, came all that *majesty* and *joy*. He *defied* his fate with JUBILATION! And I can't just sit around in my winter ash heap, wringing my hands, feeling sorry for myself, in the face of *that music*! Not only does it wipe out spiritual rot, it probably cures colds, too.

(Getting small dais/podium or chair to stand on.) Some day, some incredible December night, when I am very rich, I am going to rent me a grand hall and a great

choir and a mighty symphony orchestra. *(Places podium C.)* Stand on the podium... and conduct the Ninth. *(Rushing D enjoying the absurdity of this concept.)* And I will *personally* play the kettledrum part all the way through to the glorious end, while *simultaneously (Shouting.)* SINGING ALONG AT THE VERY TOP OF MY LUNGS!!! *(Pause, as he absorbs the power of the silence and allows it to ring for a moment. He is deeply moved.)*

And in the *awesome* silence that follows, I will bless all-the-gods-that-be, for Ludwig van Beethoven,

...for his Ninth

...and his "light."

(He crosses to the podium, steps up onto it with great anticipation. Looks at his imaginary orchestra.)

MANALIVE!

(SOUND CUE: "Ode to Joy." BRANISLAV conducts wildly, with great passion, getting goofy with joy. A strong light from the floor shines on him like a spotlight casting a huge shadow on the back wall. Lights fade to black while the music from Beethoven's Ninth gets louder as it continues in the dark. Sound fades after crest of applause.)

Note: It is very important that the precise music cues from Beethoven's Ninth be used. These specific music cues are located in the piano score and can be identified for the sound designer by the music director. Timing for final light cues is also indicated in the piano score. To

order copies of this and other sound cues on compact disc, see sound plot in appendix F.

DONNIE THE LEAF RAKER

(The peak of the applause from "Beethoven" is interrupted by the sound of pounding on a door—live offstage or taped SOUND CUE. FRED rushes onto a bare stage as though rushing to answer an emergency at the door.)

FRED. The rap on the door was sharp, urgent, insistent—a foreboding of crisis. Me, rushing to the door, fumbling with the lock, my adrenaline pumping, preparing for emergency. *(Opens the door. Expecting a disaster, he is nonplused by what he finds.)* Small boy. Odd expression. Hands me a scrawled note on much-folded paper: *(Reading the pantomimed paper.)* "My name is Donnie. I will rake your leaves. One dollar a yard. I am deaf." *(Looks at Donnie.)* "You can write to me. I can read. I rake good."

   (Stepping away from the story for a moment to give us some background. Leaf gobos fill the stage.) Now behind our house is this row of tall, middle-aged, matronly maple trees, extravagantly decked out in a million leaf-sequins. And in season the sequins detach and lie about the feet of these matrons like dressing gowns they've just stepped out of in preparation for the bath of winter.

(Unbeknownst to FRED, KATHLEEN enters.)

FRED. I like the way it looks. I like the way it looks VERY much. *(They speak directly to the audience as well as to each other.)*

KATHLEEN. His wife does not. The gardening magazine does not like it, either. Leaves should be raked. Leaves are not good for grass. Leaves are untidy. Leaves are moldy-slimy.

FRED. There is a *reason* for leaves. There is *no* reason for mowed grass, so say I.

KATHLEEN. His wife does not see it this way.

FRED. There is an unspoken accusation in the air of laziness.

KATHLEEN. We have been through this before.

FRED. But this year a bargain has been struck in the name of the Scientific Method.

KATHLEEN. Half of the yard will be properly raked.

FRED. And the other half will be left in the care of nature. Come summer, we shall see.

KATHLEEN. And so my part is raked.

FRED. And mine is not.

KATHLEEN. We will see.

FRED. Yes we will! *(KATHLEEN exits. FRED works hard to defend his point of view.)* In a way, the trees are there because of the leaves. Zillions of seeds have helicoptered out of the sky to green the earth. *(Five or six helicoptered seeds drop in from above.)* The leaves follow, to protect, and nourish the next generation of trees. But stony ground, rot, bugs, bacteria, birds, and *people (Referring to KATHLEEN.)* —all interfere. But somehow, some seeds make it. Some tenacious seeds take hold and hold on and hold on—for dear life. And they plant themselves and survive to become the next generation. This process has been going on for ages, and we mess with this process at our peril, say I. THIS IS IMPORTANT. *(Finishing his excessive defense, he is reminded of where he left off, and returns to the story.)*

"My name is Donnie. I will rake your leaves. One dollar a yard. I am deaf. You can write to me. I can read. I rake good."

He holds out the paper and pencil with patience and hope and goodwill. *(Unwilling to let go of his need to win, he is caught between a rock and a hard place.)* How can I explain to him about the importance of this scientific experiment going on in my backyard? He turns to go *(FRED makes a snap decision.)* ...and quickly I take the paper and pencil and write, *(He mimes writing.)* "Yes, I would like you to rake my leaves." *(Each time he shows the mimed paper to Donnie.)*

There is a grave nod from this attentive businessman-child.

"Do you rake them when they are wet?"

"Yes."

"Do you have your own rake?"

"No."

"This is a big yard. I think I should give you two dollars." *(The invisible Donnie responds to FRED'S generosity by upping the ante, catching FRED by surprise. FRED responds with mock outrage.)* "THREE?!"

(Charmed by Donnie's chutzpah.) We have a contract. The rake is procured, and Donnie the deaf leaf raker goes to work in the fast-falling November twilight. In silence he rakes. In silence I watch him through the window of the dark house. Are there any sounds at all in his mind? I wonder.

He rakes the leaves into a large pile, as instructed. Of course, I will spread them out over the yard again after he is gone. I am stubborn about this. *But*... he goes back over the yard picking up missed leaves by hand and carrying them to the pile. He is stubborn about *his* values. Raking the leaves means all the leaves.

He signs to me that it is getting dark and that he must go home to eat, and he leaves the work unfinished. Having paid him in advance, I wonder if he will return. At my age, I am getting cynical. *But*... come morning, he has returned to his task. And after much *meticulous* work, the yard is leaf-free.

(Charmed.) I see him stoop down and pick up some of the brightest yellow leaves and stuff them into the pocket of his sweatshirt. Along with a whole handful of helicoptered seeds. *(SOUND CUE: Door knocking.)* He reports to the door, signing that the work is done. As he walks away up the street I see him tossing one helicoptered seed into the air after another... A fringe benefit. And I stand in my own door in silence, smiling at his grace... A fringe benefit.

(One last burst of determination to stick with his plan to spread the leaves back over the yard.) Tomorrow, I will go out to the yard and I will push that pile of leaves... *(Surrendering to his heart, he changes his mind.)* ...over the embankment into the ravine behind our house. I will do it in silence. The leaves and seeds will have to work out their destiny down there this year. I wouldn't have the heart to undo his work. My scientific experiment will just have to stand aside for something more human.

The leaves have let go, the trees have let go, and now it's time for me to let go and cast my lot with this child, who like the seed is another one of nature's tenacious survivors.

Hold on, Donnie, hold on.

(As he speaks this line, he simultaneously presents it in American Sign Language. On his exit, he tosses helicoptered seeds into the air. PIANO TRANSITION.)

"THE STUFF IN THE SINK"
(The Song)

(PIANO MUSIC. FRED and KATHLEEN enter; they are the rational voices of adult maturity. The other three enter as teenagers ad-libbing loudly about the grossness of the "stuff." FRED holds a sink strainer, to which KATHLEEN refers. The following is like a "Point/Counterpoint" presentation to the audience.)

KATHLEEN *(matter-of-factly)*.
    AFTER THE DISHES ARE WASHED, THE SOAP
      RINSED AWAY,
    IN THE STRAINER AT THE BOTTOM OF THE
      SINK THERE SITS
    WHAT I WILL, FOR THE MOMENT, CALL SOME
      "STUFF."
    NOW ANY RATIONAL, OBJECTIVE PERSON
      WOULD SAY
    THIS IS SIMPLY A MIXTURE OF BITS
    OF FOOD WHICH ARE NOT SMALL ENOUGH
    TO GO DOWN THE DRAIN, COMPRISED

**OF CARBOHYDRATES, FIBER, FAT AND
PROTEIN.**

FRED. Dinner dandruff.

KATHLEEN.
**FURTHERMORE, THE PERSON MIGHT THINK
THIS STUFF HAS ALREADY BEEN STERILIZED
IN THE COOKING, AND THEN RINSED CLEAN
WITH SUDS AND HOT WATER IN THE SINK.**

FRED. No problem.

BRANISLAV (*the teens emphatically defend their point of
view*).
**BUT ANY TEEN
WHO'S EVER BEEN** (*Pronounced BEAN.*)
**FORCED TO DO THE DISHES
AGAINST HIS WISHES
WILL TESTIFY
THIS EXPLANATION'S A LIE.**
(*Using very large tongs to avoid touching the strainer,
ED takes the strainer from FRED.*)

ED.
**HE WILL PROFESS
THAT GOOEY MESS
IS A TOXIC CATASTROPHE,**
(*Passes tongs and strainer to JILL.*)

JILL.
A DEADLY CALAMITY—

JILL, ED, BRANISLAV.
> **TO ANY RATIONAL GUY OR GIRL,**
> **IT'S ENOUGH TO MAKE YOU HURL.**

KATHLEEN. Oh please, your mom deals with that stuff all the time. *(She takes strainer from tongs and mimes cleaning it out with her hands.)*

ED.
> **ABOUT MY MOM, WHATEVER ELSE I MIGHT**
> **SAY,**
> **SHE'LL REACH INTO THAT STRAINER ANY**
> **OLD DAY,**
> **AND PICK UP THAT LETHAL GUNK WITH HER**
> **BARE HANDS**...
> *(KATHLEEN casually holds up hand turning both sides to the audience for examination.)*

ED, JILL, BRANISLAV. *Bare hands!!*

ED *(KATHLEEN crosses to the trap in the floor and mimes dropping the gunk in).*
> **AND DROP IT IN THE GARBAGE, NO IFS, BUTS**
> **OR ANDS.**
> **TO TOP THAT, I ONCE SAW HER DRAG**
> **HER FINGERS THROUGH THE WET GARBAGE**
> **BAG,**
> **SEARCHING THROUGH THAT SLUDGE WITH**
> **CARE**
> **FOR AN OLD TEASPOON THAT FELL IN THERE**...

ED, JILL, BRANISLAV. *Barehanded!!!*

ED.
>A KIND OF RECKLESS BRAVERY.
>SHE FOUND THE SPOON EVENTUALLY
>*(KATHLEEN fishes way down into the trap, a light comes from within, maybe some fog suggesting the bowels of hell.)*
>IN A SOGGY CLUMP OF COFFEE DREGS
>MIXED WITH CHICKEN FAT AND SCRAMBLED EGGS,
>SOME VEGETABLE SOUP AND ACORN SQUASH.
>*(KATHLEEN terrifies ED by handing him the imaginary spoon.)*
>I ALMOST PASSED OUT WHEN SHE GAVE IT TO ME TO WASH.
>*(ED chases JILL with the grotesque pantomimed spoon.)*

BRANISLAV.
>ONCE MY FRENCH TEACHER
>HAPPENED TO FEATURE
>THE WORD "ORDURE" IN A LESSON

JILL. Ordure
ED. Ordure

BRANISLAV.
>IT MEANT "DISGUSTING MESS," AND
>LET THERE BE NO DOUBT—
>*(Points to the gunk in the strainer.)*
>I KNEW WHAT SHE WAS TALKING ABOUT.
>*(KATHLEEN hands the strainer to BRANISLAV.)*

BRANISLAV *(tossing strainer to JILL)*. Ordure
JILL *(tossing strainer to ED)*. Ordure

ED *(tossing strainer offstage)*. Ordure

BRANISLAV *(KATHLEEN and BRANISLAV mime doing the dinner dishes)*.
> I SEE THAT UGLY SIGHT
> IN THE STRAINER EVERY NIGHT.
> WHEN MY MOTHER HEARD
> MY EXCITING NEW WORD
> DURING DISHWASHING DUTY,
> SHE GAVE ME A SNOOTY
> "MY SON THE IDIOT" LOOK
> RIGHT OUT OF THE BOOK,
> AND SAID SHE HAD THE SUSPICION

that the food I had just eaten was at that very moment in my stomach in just about the same condition...ROTTING! *(He has gotten sick to his stomach.)*

JILL.
> NO MATTER WHAT MY MOTHER THINKS, IT
>   SHOULD BE STRESSED,
> THAT STUFF IS LETHAL AND SEPTIC. I'M
>   CONVINCED,
> IF YOU EVER ACCIDENTALLY TOUCH IT, YOU
>   MUST NEVER TOUCH THE REST
> OF YOUR BODY WITH YOUR HANDS UNTIL
>   YOU'VE SCALDED, SOAPED, AND RINSED.
> EVEN WORSE, I KNOW THAT LITTLE HEAP
> COULD CONGEAL AND MUTATE INTO A LIFE
>   FORM, THAT COULD CREEP
> OUT OF THE SINK AND COME AFTER YOU
>   WHEN YOU'RE ASLEEP.
(All run U to escape the lethal gunk.)

FRED (*crosses D as he speaks*). Come to think of it ...
>**MY DAD NEVER CAME WITHIN THREE FEET
>OF THE SINK IN HIS LIFE.
>HE WAS JUST LAZY, IN THE OPINION OF HIS
>WIFE.
>BUT I KNEW THAT HE KNEW WHAT I KNEW
>ABOUT THE GUNK.
>I TOLD HIM ONCE, "SOMEHOW I DOUBT
>THAT JESUS EVER HAD TO CLEAN THAT GUNK
>OUT."
>HE AGREED, MY DAD.
>IT WAS THE ONLY THEOLOGICAL DISCUSSION
>WE EVER HAD.**

(*ED, BRANISLAV, AND JILL march as if in a graduation procession, then sit C as if at commencement.
KATHLEEN and FRED move DR and DL, and address
the audience as if it were the graduation class. The teens
do not look directly at KATHLEEN and FRED, but act
as if they were seeing them off in the distance, out front.
The reactions of the students are as important as the
proclamations of the speakers.*)

KATHLEEN (*to audience, as narrator*).
>**IMAGINE A SPEAKER AT A HIGH SCHOOL
>GRADUATION.
>HE ASKS THE STUDENTS:**

FRED (*as the speaker*).
>**"HOW MANY OF YOU WOULD LIKE TO BE
>ADULTS, OUT ON YOUR OWN?"**
>(*JILL, ED and BRANISLAV raise their hands.*)

KATHLEEN.
> **ALL HANDS SHOOT UP WITHOUT HESITATION.**
> **THEN THE SPEAKER LISTS A FEW**
> **OF THE THINGS THEY WILL HAVE TO DO**
> **WHEN THEY'RE GROWN:**

(KATHLEEN and FRED each take on the persona of a very pompous speaker, with exaggerated adult authority. Each item gets louder, so they are both practically shouting by "...then you will be adults.")

FRED. <u>Clean the sink strainer.</u> *(Pause.)* <u>Plunge out the toilet.</u> *(Pause.)* <u>Clean up babies when they poop and pee.</u>

(JILL, ED and BRANISLAV begin to get queasy and reveal wide-eyed astonishment as the horrible truth unfolds. They have a hard time keeping their hands in the air.)

KATHLEEN *(pause).* <u>Wipe runny noses.</u> *(Pause.)* <u>Clean up the floor when the baby throws up strained spinach.</u>

FRED *(pause).* <u>Empty out the kitty litter.</u> *(Pause.)* <u>Scrape up the dog doo.</u>

KATHLEEN *(pause).* <u>Bury dead pets when they get run over in the street!</u>

FRED *(pause).* <u>When you can do these things, then you will be adults</u>!

(ED, JILL, and BRANISLAV are mortified and thoroughly grossed out. Their hands come down.)

KATHLEEN *(as narrator, commenting to the audience).*

**AT THIS POINT, SOME STUDENTS MAY NOT
WANT TO GO ON.
BUT SOONER OR LATER, THE TRUTH WILL
DAWN.**

FRED & KATHLEEN *(gradually getting more evangelical
in their passion).*
**THE FACT IS, MEMBERSHIP IN COMMUNITY
DEPENDS
ON OUR WILLINGNESS TO DO THESE CHORES,
MY FRIENDS.
BEING AN ADULT IS DIRTY WORK, BUT
SOMEONE HAS TO DO IT.**

*(ED, JILL, and BRANISLAV run off in panic and dis-
gust. One or more is fighting the urge to throw up.
FRED and KATHLEEN watch, then slap a "high five"
on the cut-off. PIANO TRANSITION.)*

THE STUFF IN THE SINK
(Alternate spoken version)

*(PIANO MUSIC. FRED and KATHLEEN enter; they are
rational voices of adult maturity. The other three enter
as teenagers, ad-libbing loudly about the grossness of
the "stuff." The following is like a "Point/Counterpoint"
presentation to the audience. An invisible sink is established. The cast refers to it through the first half of the
story.)*

KATHLEEN *(matter-of-factly while standing at an imagined sink).* After the dishes are washed and the sink

rinsed out, there remains in the strainer at the bottom of the sink what I will call, momentarily, some "stuff." Now, any rational, intelligent, objective person would say that this is simply a mixture of food particles too big to go down the drain, composed of bits of protein, carbohydrates, fat and fiber.

FRED. Dinner dandruff.

KATHLEEN. Furthermore, the person might add that this material was first sterilized by the high heat of cooking and further sanitized by going through the detergent and hot water of the dishpan, and rinsed.

FRED. No problem. *(KATHLEEN and FRED cross away, while the teens cross cautiously toward the imagined sink and emphatically defend their point of view to the audience.)*

BRANISLAV. But any teenager who has been forced into washing dishes knows this explanation is a lie.

ED. That stuff in the bottom of the strainer is toxic waste.

JILL. Deadly poison.

ED. A danger to health.

BRANISLAV. In other words, it's about enough to make you hurl.

KATHLEEN. Oh please, your mom deals with that stuff all the time.

ED *(referring to imagined sink)*. One of the very few reasons I have any respect for my mother at all is because she reaches into the sink with her bare hands—BARE HANDS—and picks up that lethal gunk and drops it into the garbage. To top that, I saw her reach into the wet garbage bag and fish around in there looking for a lost teaspoon BAREHANDED—a kind of *unbelievable* courage. She found the spoon in a clump of coffee grounds mixed with chicken fat and scrambled eggs. I almost passed out when she gave it to me to wash.

BRANISLAV. Once, in French class, we learned the word "ordure," and when the teacher told me it meant "unspeakable filth," I knew exactly what she was talking about. I see it every night. *(Referring to the imagined sink.)* In the bottom of the sink.

That night at dishwashing time, I told my mother "we have *ordure* in our sink." Well, she gave me her "my-son-the-idiot" look and explained that the dinner I had just eaten was at that very moment in my stomach, in just about the same condition ... ROTTING!!! *(He has gotten sick to his stomach.)*

JILL *(referring to imagined sink).* No matter what my mother thinks, I know that the stuff in the sink strainer is lethal and septic. It will give you leprosy or something worse. If you should ever accidentally touch it, you must never touch any other part of your body with your fingers until you have scalded and soaped and rinsed your hands. Even worse, I know that the "stuff" can congeal and mush up and mutate into some living thing that can crawl out of the sink during the night and get loose in the house. *(The boys sneak up behind JILL, scaring her. They all run away from the sink.)*

FRED *(seeing their point for a moment, speaks to audience).* Come to think of it, my father never came closer than three feet to the sink in his life. My mother said he was lazy. But I knew that he knew what I knew about the gunk. I told him once, "I bet Jesus never had to wash dishes and clean the gunk out of the sink." He agreed. It was the only theological discussion we ever had.

(PIANO MUSIC: "Pomp and Circumstance." The teens march as if in a graduation procession, then sit C as if at commencement. KATHLEEN and FRED moved DR and DL and address the audience as if it were the graduating class. The teens do not look directly at KATHLEEN and FRED, but act as if they were seeing them off in the distance, out front. The reactions of the students are as important as the proclamations of the speakers.)

KATHLEEN *(to audience as narrator)*. Imagine a high school graduation speech. The speaker addresses the students and asks,

FRED *(as graduation speaker)*. "How many of you would like to be adults, independent, on-your-own citizens?" *(The teens, as graduates, raise their hands.)*

KATHLEEN. Well, all hands would go up with some enthusiasm. And the speaker would then give them this list of things that grown-ups do:

(KATHLEEN and FRED each take on the persona of a pompous speaker, with exaggerated adult authority. Each item gets louder so that they are both practically shouting by "..then you will be adults.")

FRED. Clean the sink strainer.

KATHLEEN *(pause)*. Plunge out the toilet.

FRED *(pause)*. Clean up babies when they poop and pee.

(JILL, ED and BRANISLAV begin to get queasy and reveal wide-eyed astonishment as the horrible truth un-

folds. Mortified, they have a hard time keeping their hands in the air, but try.)

KATHLEEN *(pause).* Wipe runny noses. *(Pause.)* Clean up the floor when the baby throws up strained spinach.

FRED *(pause).* Empty out the kitty litter. *(Pause.)* Scrape up dog doo.

KATHLEEN *(pause).* Bury dead pets when they get run over in the street.

FRED *(pause).* When you can do these things, then you will be adults! *(The students' hands finally drop completely.)*

KATHLEEN *(as the narrator from the beginning of the story).* Some of the students may not want to go on at this point. But they may as well face the truth. Taking out the garbage of this life is a condition of membership in community.

FRED *(with evangelical fervor).* BEING AN ADULT IS DIRTY WORK!!!

KATHLEEN *(with equal evangelical fervor).* BUT SOMEONE HAS TO DO IT!!!

(ED, having turned green, dashes offstage holding his mouth, while JILL and BRANISLAV exit in disgust waving their hands. KATHLEEN and FRED watch them exit, then cross C with mock pomp, which is broken by a "high-five" slap as they dash off triumphantly. Lights fade to transition. PIANO TRANSITION.)

PROBLEMS AND INCONVENIENCES

(ED enters with single chair, places it and sits C by the final chord of the transition music from "Stuff in the Sink." A pool of light comes up on him. SOUND CUE: Summer crickets, softly under the entire story.)

ED. Summer of 1959 at the Feather River Inn near the town of Blairsden in the Sierra Nevada Mountains of northern California. A resort community. And I...

(BRANISLAV enters as the young ED; he stays unobtrusively busy with a clipboard U. ED only casually refers to him.)

...just out of college, have a job that combines being the night desk clerk in the lodge and helping out with the horse-wrangling at the stables. The owner/manager is Italian-Swiss, with European notions about conditions of employment. He and I do not get along. I think he's a fascist who wants peasant employees who know their place, and he thinks I'm a good example of how democracy can be carried too far.

One week the employees had been served the same thing for lunch every single day. Two wieners, a mound of sauerkraut, and stale rolls. To compound insult with injury, the cost of meals was deducted from our check. I was outraged. *(ED rises.)*

On Friday night of that awful week, I was at my desk job around eleven o'clock and the night auditor had just come on duty.

*(FRED enters as Sigmund, sits on stool R; BRANISLAV
exits in the other direction to kitchen.)*

I went into the kitchen to get a bite to eat and found
notes to the chef to the effect that wieners and sauerkraut were on the employee menu for two more days.

BRANISLAV *(shouting from offstage).* THAT TEARS IT! I
QUIT!

ED. For want of any better audience, I unloaded on the
night auditor, Sigmund Wollman.

*(BRANISLAV storms on. ED begins to view and dodge
the irate youth. Neither FRED nor BRANISLAV ever acknowledge ED's presence.)*

BRANISLAV *(outraged, and ridiculously indignant. FRED
barely reacts).* I have had it up to here! I am going to
get a plate of wieners and sauerkraut, wake up the owner
and throw it on him! I am sick and tired of this crap, and
insulted, and nobody is going to make me eat wieners
and sauerkraut for a whole week and make me pay for
it! Who does he think he is, anyhow?! How can life be
sustained on wieners and sauerkraut?! This is un-Ameri-
can! And I don't like wieners and sauerkraut enough to
eat it one day, for God's sake! And the whole hotel
stinks anyhow! And the horses are all nags! And all the
guests are idiots! And I'm packing my bags and heading
for Montana, where they never even heard of wieners
and sauerkraut, and wouldn't feed that stuff to pigs!!!

ED *(recognizing all too well what a total jerk he used to
be).* Something like that. I raved on this way for twenty

minutes, and needn't repeat it all here. You get the drift. My monologue was delivered at the top of my lungs.

BRANISLAV *(simultaneously with ED).* THE TOP OF MY LUNGS.

ED. Punctuated by blows...

BRANISLAV *(overlapping).* BLOWS ON THE FRONT DESK,

ED. ...the kicking of chairs, *(ED rescues the chair just as BRANISLAV starts to kick it.)*

BRANISLAV. AND MUCH PROFANITY!

ED. A call to arms,

BRANISLAV *(at a fevered pitch, like a rallying cry).* FREEDOM, UNIONS, UPRISINGS AND THE BREAKING OF CHAINS FOR THE WORKING MASSES!!!

ED. As I pitched my fit, Sigmund Wollman, the night auditor, sat watching me with sorrowful eyes. Put a bloodhound in a suit and you have Sigmund Wollman. *(Casual and matter-of-fact, but with respect and affection.)* He's got good reason to look sorrowful. Survivor of Auschwitz. Three years. German Jew. He liked being alone at the night job—gave him intellectual space, gave him peace and quiet, and even more, he could go into the kitchen and have a snack whenever he wanted to— all the wieners and sauerkraut he wanted. To him, a feast. More than that, there's nobody around at night to tell him what to do. In Auschwitz he dreamed of such a time. The only person he sees at work is me... *(Referring to BRANISLAV.)* the nightly disturber of his dream. Our shifts overlap for an hour. And here I am again. A one-man war party at full cry.

BRANISLAV *(one last screech of frustration).* AAAAHH-HHHHhhhhhhhhh!!!!!!!!!!!!!!!!

FRED. Are you finished?

BRANISLAV. No! Why?!

FRED (*with appropriate dialect*). Lissen, lissen to me. You know what's wrong with you? It's not wieners and kraut and it's not the boss and it's not the chef and it's not this job.

BRANISLAV. What's wrong with me?

FRED (*with stern patriarchal clarity, and a degree of compassion for this young man's growth*). You think you know everything, but you don't know the difference between an inconvenience and a problem. If you break your neck, if you have nothing to eat, if your house is on fire, you got a problem. Everything else is just inconvenience. Life is inconvenient. Life is *lumpy*. You learn to know the difference between an inconvenience and a problem. You'll live longer. And you won't annoy people like me so much. Good night. (*FRED exits UR, waving his hand in a gesture of dismissal; BRANISLAV exits DL.*)

ED (*alone on chair C in a small pool of light as in opening*). There in the late-night darkness of the Feather River Inn, Sigmund Wollman simultaneously kicked my butt and opened a window in my mind. Problem or inconvenience? I call this the Wollman Test of Reality. Life is lumpy. But a lump in the oatmeal—a lump in the throat —and a lump in the breast—are not the same lump. We should learn to know the difference. Good night, Sig.

(*PIANO TRANSITION.*)

THE BENCH

(BRANISLAV places a bench C and exits. JILL enters and stands off to the side.)

JILL. There is a bench in the city where I live. Its structure is simple—three slabs of smooth gray granite. And, having checked with a compass to be certain, I can tell you that this bench has been carefully placed so that the long sides face east and west and the short ends point north and south.

(Cloud gobos come up as she takes stage, drinking in the magnificent setting she is describing.) This sturdy seat has been placed with purpose on the highest ground of the highest hill in the city. So that when the sky is clear on a summer's morning, you can see almost sixty miles in three directions.

This bench is, in fact, a tombstone in a cemetery. *(PI-ANO MUSIC underscores till the end.)* And I would take you there to sit if I could.

You wouldn't feel uncomfortable sitting on it, I promise. You wouldn't even notice what it was at first. It's right on the edge of a paved lane that curves through the burial grounds. It's placed so that you are clearly invited to use it. The placement of the bench, the consciousness of the view—all say that someone went to a lot of trouble to be useful in death. A parting gesture of quiet generosity has been made.

Funerals have a certain narcissism to them, a focus on self: what I want for MY funeral and what I want for MY epitaph—a very human holding on to identity as long as breath and granite last. But to me, tombstones are markers of loneliness.

But this bench is another story. Unique. First of all, there's no name inscribed on it. No conventional epitaph. No dates. Just an open invitation to sit and think. *(She sits and enjoys a moment of silence.)* What marks this grave is the gift of silent companionship that bridges loneliness.

This bench has become a spiritual retreat for me over the years. And I know that I am not the only one to use it, because once I found a note taped under the bench. Not for me: for a young woman from a young man who was in love with her and wrote her careless poetry with great passion. And no, I'm not sorry I snooped; and yes, I put it back as I found it; and no, I didn't hide in the bushes and wait and see who came for the note. Secret lovers have enough problems as it is.

But it was on this bench, the summer morning after one of those "milestone" birthdays, that I came to that moment when one crosses over from the abstract intellectual knowledge that all human beings die ... to the active realization that *I* will die. *Me.* I will not be. Sooner or later.

Not only did I realize that I will die, but I walked away thinking ... well ... It's OK.

I connect that moment of enlightenment with the peculiar sanctuary of the bench and whoever provided it. This bench will last hundreds of years. Many people will sit on it and think not of the name of its owner but of the nameless joys of this *sweet* life ...

and the mystery of death ...

and how utterly *amazing* it all is.

And that somehow...

sometimes...

things are *just* as they should be.

(PIANO SEGUE.)

"REFLECT THE LIGHT"

(As JILL sits on the bench, thinking, BRANISLAV enters, drinks in the moment, and begins to sing. He does not acknowledge her at first.)

BRANISLAV.
    IT IS A SWEET LIFE,
      WHEN I TAKE THE TIME TO SEE IT;
    AND THERE IS WONDER INSIDE ME,
      IF I CAN FIND A WAY TO FREE IT.
    SOMETIMES IT SEEMS SO EASY
      TO WALK THROUGH MY LIFE
    WITH MY EYES CLOSED
      TO HEARTACHE AND STRIFE—
    BUT EVERY SO OFTEN,
      EVEN IN MY MIND'S DARKEST NIGHT,
    THERE COMES, STREAMING THROUGH MY
      WINDOW,
      A FRAGMENT OF LIGHT,
    A GLIMPSE OF TRUTH
      FOR ME TO PARTAKE—
    AND I MIGHT MISS IT
      IF I'M NOT AWAKE.

    HOW CAN I LIVE IN THE DARK,

WHEN I COULD BE PART OF THAT LIGHT?
HOW DO I CAPTURE THAT SPARK
AND REFLECT IT INTO THE HEART OF THE
   NIGHT?

(The others enter, as he crosses and sits beside JILL on the bench.)

THERE'S NO WAY TO MEASURE
   WHAT THESE FRAGMENTS ARE WORTH—
SCATTERED MOMENTS OF CONNECTION
   TO LIFE ON THIS EARTH;
FLASHES OF UNDERSTANDING,
   THAT CAN SET YOUR SOUL ABLAZE
AND FLICKER SOFTLY
   THROUGH ALL OF YOUR DAYS.

(Rising.)
   STOP NOW AND LISTEN.
      CAN YOU HEAR A FAINT MELODY?
   JUST OUTSIDE HERE,

ALL.
   ALL AROUND US
   A GREAT SYMPHONY.

BRANISLAV.	ALL.
BUT NOTHING IN LIFE	OOH ...
HAS THE POWER TO INSPIRE	
LIKE ADDING YOUR OWN VOICE	AHH ...
TO THE MIGHTY CHOIR.	

ALL.
> **HOW CAN WE LIVE IN THE DARK,**
> **WHEN WE COULD BE PART OF THAT LIGHT?**
> **HOW DO WE CAPTURE THAT SPARK**
> **AND REFLECT IT INTO THE HEART OF THE**
> **NIGHT?**

(Optional extension with BRANISLAV improvising above others. See score.)

ALL.
> **I WANNA REFLECT, REFLECT THE LIGHT.**
> **I WANNA REFLECT, REFLECT THE LIGHT.**
> **I WANNA REFLECT REFLECT THE LIGHT.**
> **INTO THE HEART OF THE NIGHT.**

END ACT ONE

ACT TWO

"UH-OH"
(The Song)

(The cast enters and stands in formal choral formation. The pianist enters in tails, with a conductor's baton, and bows. Tongue-in-cheek, they give the appearance of a formal concert. The pianist/conductor is required to return to the piano just before the musical accompaniment begins. If the piano is not easily accessible to him/her, the rhythm choruses can be performed without a conductor, or with one of the cast members conducting.)

(RHYTHM CHORUS Part 1—Spoken.)

KATHLEEN. Uh-oh.
JILL. Oops!
BRANISLAV. Ouch!
FRED. Hmph!
KATHLEEN. Uh-oh.
ED. Unh-unh.
BRANISLAV. Ow!
JILL. Oops!
KATHLEEN. Yikes!
ED. Hunh?
FRED. Hmph!
KATHLEEN. Uh-oh.

ED. Eek!

BRANISLAV. Hunh!

ED. Unh-unh.

BRANISLAV. Ouch!

JILL. Oops!

FRED. Ugh!

KATHLEEN. Uh-oh.

BRANISLAV. Ick!

KATHLEEN & FRED. Uh-oh.

JILL. Pew!

KATHLEEN, BRANISLAV, FRED. Uh-oh.

ED. Sheesh!

JILL, KATHLEEN, BRANISLAV, FRED. Uh-oh.

KATHLEEN. Yikes!

JILL, BRANISLAV, ED, FRED. Uh-oh.

FRED. Ewww!

JILL, KATHLEEN, BRANISLAV, ED. Uh-oh.

BRANISLAV. Whoa!

JILL, KATHLEEN, ED, FRED. Uh-oh.

JILL. Awww!

KATHLEEN, BRANISLAV, ED, FRED. Uh-oh.

ALL. YUCK! *(Pianist crosses to piano to start accompaniment.)* Uh-oh, uh-oh, uh-oh, uh-oh, uh-oh, uh-oh, uh-oh, uh-oh, uh-oh,uh-oh, uh-oh.

(End RHYTHM CHORUS Part 1.)

ED.
UH-OH ISN'T IN THE DICTIONARY—

BRANISLAV.
YOU HARDLY EVER SEE IT ON THE PAGE—

FRED.
> BUT IT'S PART OF OUR VOCABULARY,

ED.
> AND HAS BEEN SINCE THE DIAPER AGE.

ALL.
> UH-OH:

JILL *(pantomimes handing an apple to ED).*
> WHAT DID ADAM SAY TO EVIE
> MOMENTS AFTER HE BEGAN TO CHEW
> ON THE APPLE SHE GAVE HIM?
> WELL, I BELIEVE HE
> SAID

ED *(speaks as if with a mouthful of apple).*
> "UH-OH."

JILL.
> AND SHE UNDERSTOOD HIM, TOO.

ALL.
> MILLIONS OF SOUNDS HAVE COME AND GONE
>   THROUGHOUT HISTORY,
> AS WE'VE REACHED FOR WAYS TO
>   COMMUNICATE MORE EFFECTIVELY.

KATHLEEN.
> THE MOST POTENT WORDS WE USE, IN MANY
>   CASES,
> HAVE BEEN GRUNTS AND MOANS,

ED.
> **TOGETHER WITH SHRUGS AND FUNNY FACES.**

JILL. Nya Nya Nya-Nya Nya.
FRED. Boo!
BRANISLAV. Nuh-unh!
ED. Neenor Neenor Neenor!
KATHLEEN *(sarcastically)*. Ha Ha Ha.
FRED *(blows razzberry)*.

ALL.
> **UH-OH,**

BRANISLAV.
> **QUIETLY REVERBERATING**
> **SINCE ADAM'S TIME, IS PART OF A SYMPHONY**
> **OF SQUEAKS AND SQUAWKS,**
>   **COMMUNICATING**
> **ELABORATE THOUGHTS WITH PERFECT**
>   **CLARITY.**

(RHYTHM CHORUS PART 2—Spoken.)

FRED. Hmph!
KATHLEEN. Uh-oh, uh-oh.
JILL. Oops!
KATHLEEN. Uh-oh.
ED. Ouch!
KATHLEEN. Uh-oh.
FRED. Hunh.
BRANISLAV. Sheesh!
JILL. Ick!
KATHLEEN. Uh-oh.

ED. Ow!

KATHLEEN. Uh-oh.

BRANISLAV. Yikes!

JILL. Pew!

FRED. Ugh!

KATHLEEN. Uh-oh, uh-oh.

ED. Annh.

KATHLEEN. Uh-oh.

JILL. Ewww!

KATHLEEN. Uh-oh.

BRANISLAV. Owww!

KATHLEEN. Uh-oh.

ED. Awww!

KATHLEEN. Uh-oh.

FRED. Whoa!

KATHLEEN. Uh-oh.

ALL. Hunh.

JILL & KATHLEEN. Ha!

FRED. Ooh.

ED. Unh-hunh.

BRANISLAV. Whew.

FRED. Hmmm...

KATHLEEN. Aha!

JILL. Hunh.

ED & FRED. Wow!

BRANISLAV. Ah.

KATHLEEN. Oh.

JILL. Ooh.

ED. Unh-hunh.

BRANISLAV. Whew.

JILL & KATHLEEN. Mm-mm-mm!

BRANISLAV. Yay!

KATHLEEN. Yippee!

FRED. Ha!

KATHLEEN. Yippee!

ED. Yowza!

KATHLEEN. Yippee!

BRANISLAV. Weee!

FRED. Wow!

JILL. Yum!

KATHLEEN. Hooray!

ED. Yahoo!

BRANISLAV. Yee-ha!

FRED. Wonga wonga wonga wonga wonga...

BRANISLAV *(wolf whistle).*

FRED *(simultaneously).* ...wonga wonga wonga...

ED & FRED. ...wonga wonga wonga wonga.

BRANISLAV. Hubba hubba hubba hubba...

BRANISLAV, ED, FRED. ...hubba hubba hubba hubba!
  (Women react to the men's wolf calling.)

KATHLEEN. Yada yada yada yada.

BRANISLAV. Hunh?

ED. Oops.

FRED. Hmph.

BRANISLAV & ED. Uh-oh.

JILL. Blah, blah, blah, blah.

ED. Hunh?

KATHLEEN. Annh.

JILL. Sheesh!

KATHLEEN. Hardy har har!

JILL. Duh!

(Pause. Continuing in sequence, they each go through a five-part thought process which leads to an "Ah-ha! discovery.")

JILL. Ho hum.
KATHLEEN. Ho hum.
BRANISLAV. Ho hum.
ED. Ho hum.
FRED. Ho hum.
  (Reacting to new information.)
JILL. Hunh?
KATHLEEN. Hunh?
BRANISLAV. Hunh?
ED. Hunh?
FRED. Hunh?
  (Alarmed at further information.)
JILL. Uh-oh.
KATHLEEN. Uh-oh.
BRANISLAV. Uh-oh.
ED. Uh-oh.
FRED. Uh-oh.
  (Processing all the information.)
JILL. Unh-hunh.
KATHLEEN. Unh-hunh.
BRANISLAV. Unh-hunh.
ED. Unh-hunh.
FRED. Unh-hunh.
  (Beginning to see the light.)
JILL. Oh, wow!
KATHLEEN. Oh, wow!
BRANISLAV. Oh, wow!
ED. Oh, wow!

FRED. Oh, wow!

(Delighted and fulfilled by the final discovery.)

ALL. Aha!

(The conductor takes a series of "maestro" bows; then tongue-in-cheek, he/she humbly presents the singers to the audience for a bow, then bows again. They exit leaving ED alone onstage. Note: if the ensemble version of MOTB is being performed, they all remain onstage. "The Wedding March" can be played as a SOUND CUE if it takes too long for the conductor to travel back to the PIANO.)

UH-OH!

(Alternate spoken version)

(The cast enters and stands in formal choral formation. The pianist enters in tails, with a conductor's baton, and bows. Tongue-in-cheek, they give the appearance of a formal concert. On the conductor's cue, they launch into a spoken rhythm chorus of simple syllable words, such as uh-oh, oops, yuck, hmph, etc. See RHYTHM CHORUS Part 1 of "Uh-Oh the song" in this script, for exact spoken words and sounds; see the piano score for exact rhythms. Substitute the following dialogue for the sung lines in the song.)

ED. Across the history of the human family ...

BRANISLAV. ...millions and millions of distinct sounds have come and gone ...

FRED. ...as we keep reaching for ways to communicate with one another.

KATHLEEN. Think of how Adam...

JILL. ...may have expressed himself to Eve, *(Pantomiming handing ED an apple.)* after *he* bit into the apple.

ED *(pantomimes biting, then speaks as if with a mouthful of apple)*. Uh-oh!

JILL. She knew exactly what he meant, too.

KATHLEEN. Ever since then...

FRED. ...humankind has been composing...

BRANISLAV. ...a symphony...

JILL. ...of short syllables...

ED. ...that represent complex thoughts.

(They resume with an extended version of the spoken "Uh-Oh rhythm chorus." See RHYTHM CHORUS Part 2 of "Uh-Oh the song" in this script for exact spoken words and sounds. See piano score for exact rhythms. At the end of the RHYTHM CHORUS Part 2, the conductor takes a series of "maestro" bows, then, tongue-in-cheek, he humbly presents the singers to the audience for a bow, then bows again. They exit leaving ED alone on-stage. Note: If the ensemble version of MOTB is being performed, they all remain onstage. "The Wedding March" can be played as a SOUND CUE if it takes too long for the conductor to travel back to the piano.)

MOTB

(PIANO MUSIC: "Here Comes The Bride" as intro. Note: There is a full ensemble version of MOTB in Appendix E.

FRED, JILL, KATHLEEN, and BRANISLAV exit, leaving ED onstage with four chairs. ED takes the point of view of a neighbor and/or close friend of the family of the bride. He puts on a navy blue blazer for the occasion.)

ED. Most weddings are such comedies. *(Long pause.)* Not that they are intended as such. But since weddings are high state occasions involving amateurs under pressure, everything NEVER goes right.

(He takes one chair and places it DLC as a representation of the MOTB. He never moves this chair again, and uses it to refer to her throughout the story.)

The central figure in this drama was the mother of the bride, the MOTB. Not the bride and groom or minister. Mother. Usually a polite, reasonable, intelligent, and sane human being, Mother was mentally unhinged by the announcement of her daughter's betrothal. I don't mean she was unhappy, as is often the case. To the contrary. She was overcome with joy. And just about succeeded in overcoming everybody else with her joy.

Nobody knew it, but this lady had been waiting with a script for a production that would have met with Cecil B. DeMille's approval. A royal wedding fit for a princess bride. The father of the bride began to pray for an elopement.

She had seven months to work and no detail was left to chance or human error. *(He gets three other chairs and sets them up during the following, suggesting pews for the two sides of the church. One front chair is for the MOTB, the other is for the mother of the groom. The other two chairs suggest pews a little further back in the church. There is a center aisle.)* Everything that could be engraved was engraved. There were teas and showers and dinners. An eighteen-piece brass-and-wind ensemble was engaged. The bride and groom met with the minister only three times—the MOTB was in his office more than the cleaning lady. Not only were the bridesmaids' outfits made to order, but the tuxedos for the groom and his men were *bought*—not rented, mind you. *Bought.* *(He is finished setting up the church.)* And, if all that wasn't enough, the engagement ring was returned to the jeweler for a larger stone—quietly subsidized by the MOTB. When I say the lady came unhinged, I mean UN-HINGED. *(PIANO CUE: Roll.)*

The juggernaut of fate rolled down the road, and the final hour came.

(PIANO MUSIC: Fanfare as ED grabs the end of a white bridal aisle runner, which has been preset D, and unfurls it so that a church aisle is established from D to U. He places the U edge of the runner on the cut-off of the musical fanfare. The fanfare and unfurling should complete before he speaks again. PIANO MUSIC underscores much of the remainder of the story.)

Guests in formal attire packed the church. Enough candles were lit to bring daylight back to the evening. In the choir loft the orchestra gushed great music. *(PIANO MUSIC.)* And the mighty MOTB coasted down the aisle with the grandeur of an opera diva at a premier performance. *(After the line, he imitates the MOTB walking down the aisle, strutting, sneaking waves to her friends, etc., and finally taking her seat.)* Never did the mother of the bride take her seat with more satisfaction. She had done it. She glowed ... beamed ... smiled ... and sighed.

(He rises to narrate the following as he paints a vivid picture. He helps us see all the action and characters against the backdrop of his church set.) The music softened, and nine—count them, nine—chiffon-draped bridesmaids lockstepped down the long aisle, while the groom and his men marched into place.

Finally, the wedding march thundered from the orchestra! *(PIANO MUSIC.)* Here comes the bride! Preceded by four enthusiastic mini-princesses chunking flower petals, and two munchkin ring bearers—one for each ring.

The congregation rose and turned in anticipation.

"Ah, the bride."

She had been dressed for hours ... if not days.

No adrenaline was left in her body.

(Putting the picture on hold, and stepping out of the world of the church, he takes the audience to the reception hall and suggests the following.) Left alone with her father in the reception hall of the church while the march of the maidens went on and on, she had walked along the tables loaded with gourmet goodies and absentmindedly sampled first the little pink and yellow and green mints. Then she picked through the silver bowls of mixed

nuts and ate the pecans. Followed by a cheeseball or two, some black olives, a handful of glazed almonds, a little sausage with a frilly toothpick stuck in it, a couple of shrimps blanketed in bacon, and a cracker piled with liver paté. To wash this down—a glass of pink champagne. Her father gave it to her. To calm her nerves.

(He returns to the moment in the church.) What you noticed as the bride stood in the doorway was not her dress, but her face. White. For what was coming down the aisle was a living grenade with the pin pulled out. *(Pause.)* The bride *(Music stops.)* ...threw up. *(Pause.)* Just as she walked by her mother. *(Pause.)* And by "threw up," I don't mean a polite little ladylike urp into her handkerchief. *(Pause.)* She *puked. (Pause.)* There's just no nice word for it. I mean, she *hosed* the front of the chancel— *(Pause.)* —hitting two bridesmaids, the groom, a ring bearer, and the minister. *(Pause.)* I am quite sure of the details. We have it all on videotape. *(Pause.)* Three cameras' worth. *(Pause.)* The MOTB had thought of everything.

Having disgorged her hors d'oeuvres, champagne, and the last of her dignity, the bride went limp in her father's arms, while her groom sat down on the floor where he had been standing, too stunned to function. And the mother of the bride moaned, slumped over and passed out cold. *(Indicates mother slumping over in rag-doll disarray.)*

There was a fire drill then and there at the front of the church that only the Marx Brothers could have topped. *(With quick movement suggesting the frenzy of the keystone cops. PIANO MUSIC.)* Groomsmen rushed about heroically, mini-princess flower girls squalled, bridesmaids sobbed, and people with weak stomachs headed for the exits. *(The action stops as the music slows down*

suggesting the wafting of the smell.) The smell ... of fresh
retch ... drifted across the church.

Only two people were seen smiling. One was *(Indicating the front pew chair for the mother of the groom.)*
... the mother of the groom. *(Pause.)* And the other ... was
the father of the bride. *(Indicating the father standing
beside his wife.)*

What happened next? Well, we all went back to real
life. Guests were invited to adjourn to the reception hall,
though they did not eat or drink as much as they might
have in different circumstances. The bride was consoled,
cleaned up, fitted out with a bridesmaid's dress, and
hugged and kissed a lot by the groom. She'll always
love him for that. When he said "For better or worse,"
he meant it. *(PIANO MUSIC.)* The cast was reassembled
where we left off, a single flute played a quiet air, the
words were spoken and the deed was done. Everybody
cried, as people are supposed to do at weddings, mostly
because the groom held the bride in his arms through the
whole ceremony. And no groom ever kissed a bride more
"tenderly" than he.

If one can hope for a wedding that it be memorable,
then theirs was a raging success. NOBODY who was there
will EVER forget it. *(He strikes the bridal runner.)*

They lived as happily ever after as anyone does—happier than most, in fact. They have been married about
twelve years now, and have three lively children.

But that's not the end of the story. *(As he talks, he
arranges the chairs into a living-room formation in front
of imaginary TV sets, keeping the same designated chair
for the MOTB in its original spot.)* On the tenth anniversary of this disastrous affair, a party was held. A feast

was laid, best friends invited, and three TV sets were mustered. Remember there were three video cameras at the scene of the accident. All three tapes were shown at once. The effect was...pretty interesting. Especially with the running commentary and the stop-action stuff that is a little gross when seen one frame at a time. The part that got cheers and toasts was when the camera focused on the grin of the father of the bride as he contemplates his wife being revived.

I really like this part of the story, not because of the party, but because of who organized it. *(Gesturing to her sitting in her chair.)* Of course. The infamous MOTB. The mother of the bride is still at it, but she's a lot looser these days. She not only forgave her husband and everybody else for their part in the debacle, she forgave herself. And nobody laughed harder at the videotapes than she.

There's a word for what she has. Grace.

And that's why that same grinning man has been married to her for forty years. And why her daughter loves her still.

(PIANO MUSIC: Wedding recessional, as ED exits, tossing a handful of rice into the audience.)

FATHERS AND SONS

(PIANO MUSIC on entrance of each actor. BRANISLAV enters carrying baseball cap.)

BRANISLAV. This is 1963. *(As narrator/observer, he paints and comments on the following picture.)* From deep in the canyoned aisles of a supermarket comes what sounds like a small-scale bus wreck *(Bus wreck sounds from PIANO.)* followed by an air raid. *(Air raid sounds from PIANO.)* If you followed the running box-boy armed with mop and broom, you would come upon a young father...his three-year-old son...an upturned shopping cart...and a good part of the pickles shelf—all in a heap on the floor. *(PIANO thud.)*

The child, who is not hurt, sits in a small lake of pickle juice and is experiencing what might nicely be described as "significant fluid loss." *Tears*...mixed with *mucus* from a runny nose...mixed with *blood* from a small forehead abrasion...mixed with *saliva* drooling from a mouth that is wide open and making a *noise* that would drive a dog under a bed.

The father has remained amazingly quiet and still in the face of this catastrophe. *(He puts on the baseball cap, becoming the father. He smiles passively, attempting to remain inconspicuous in front of the crowd. But every muscle in his body is tense with panic.)*

The father is calm because he is thinking about running away from home. Thinking about just quietly turning and walking away, since no one knows this is his kid. Getting into the car, driving away to California maybe. Changing his name. Getting a job as a paperboy or a cook in an all-night diner. Something—anything—that does not involve contact with three-year-olds!

Oh sure, someday he may find all this amusing, but in the most private part of his heart, he is sorry he has children—sorry he married—sorry he grew up—and above all, sorry that this particular son cannot be traded in for a model that works!

(Sincerely.) He will not and cannot say these things to anybody, ever, but they are there. And they are not funny. *(PIANO MUSIC.)*

Later, the father sits in his car in the parking lot holding the sobbing child in his arms until he falls asleep. He drives home and carries the child up to his crib and tucks him in. The father looks at the sleeping child for a long time. *(All his frustration melts away, revealing the depth of his love.)* The father does not run away from home.

(PIANO MUSIC. ED enters. BRANISLAV tosses cap to ED and sits DR.)

ED. This is 1976. The same father paces his living room. *(ED puts on cap, becoming the father, who is trying to cover his agitation.)* In his hand is what's left of a letter—crumpled into a ball and uncrumpled again. The letter is from his sixteen-year-old son—the same son from the pickle juice. The pride of his father's eye—or *was*, until today's mail.

The tables have turned—now it's the son who is running away from home. He says he hates his father and wishes he never had one. He says the father is a jackass, a jerk and a failure as a parent. And ends with "You can kiss my ass and drop dead."

The father is shouting at the ceiling, "WHY ME? WHY ME? WHY ME?"

Well, the answer is simple—he has a son. *(Pause.)* The son is sixteen. *(Pause.)* Shit happens. *(Pause. PIANO MUSIC.)*

Someday, some long day from now—he may laugh about even this. *(Genuinely hurt.)* But for the moment, there is only anguish.

(PIANO MUSIC. FRED enters. ED tosses cap to FRED and sits.)

FRED. This is 1988. Same father. Same son. And they are still running—out jogging at six a.m. The son is twenty-eight now, married, with his own three-year-old son. *(After a pause, he releases a big laugh of mock vindictive glee.)* The father is fifty. *(FRED puts on cap, becoming the father. Adjust fifty to sixty if appropriate.)*

As the father and son cross the busy street, the son looks both ways, with his hand on his father's elbow *(Amused by his son's misperception of his age.)* ...to hold him back from the danger of oncoming traffic. You can hear them laugh as they run on up the hill into the morning. And when they sprint toward home, the son does not run ahead...but runs alongside his father at his father's pace.

They love each other a lot. You can see that. They have been through a lot together. So they work to take care of their love. *(PIANO MUSIC.)*

ED. Oh, there will be times when they will be mad at each other again.

BRANISLAV. And there will be times when they love each other.

FRED. And one of their *favorite* stories will always be...

FRED, BRANISLAV, ED. "Once upon a time...in a supermarket!"

(BRANISLAV pats FRED on the shoulder and begins to exit. ED also pats FRED on the shoulder, expressing some unspoken and somewhat patronizingly affectionate respect for the elder FRED. ED starts to exit but turns back for a final patting. This business is a set-up for FRED's next line. ED and BRANISLAV finally exit, leaving FRED alone onstage.)

PIGEONS

FRED *(standing C).* There are little clues that my life is entering a new stage. My children are beginning to look middle-aged. *(Pause.)* And they pat me. *(Pause.)* A lot. *(Pause.)* In a very patronizing manner for no apparent reason. I'm not going to ask them why they pat me. I'll take all the affection I can get from them in any way they want to dish it up.

But another clue of change is a sudden desire to take small children on excursions.

My granddaughter, Sarah, and I went on an adventure that sounds like the title of a B-grade children's storybook. "Grandfather and Granddaughter Go to the Zoo." First time. *(Indicating the day's activities at the zoo.)* And we saw the lions and the tigers and the elephants and the giraffes and the kangaroos and the bears and the gorillas and all the rest—every last living creature the zoo had to offer and even some possible dead ones.

But for all my "Oh, Sarah, look at the..." Sarah was most impressed with the *pigeons*...that hung around the concession stand. What she liked about the pigeons was that she could almost touch them but not quite. No matter how carefully, cautiously, quietly, she approached, the pigeons always managed to stay just one small step further out of reach. The space between her and the pigeons moved in concert and she spent most of the time at the zoo trying to close this moving space. All the rest of the animals were *over there*, behind bars or moats or glass, in another world. But the pigeons were *over here*, in her world, and would be made even more real if she could just get her hands on one.

"Well, what would you do with it if you caught one, Sarah?"

She didn't know. Possessing was not in the plan. Just reaching for the pigeons was all that mattered to her.

(SOUND CUE: Thunder. FRED gets a chair and sits angled UL. He looks over his shoulder to the car seat behind him, facing the audience. He is in a pool of light.)

Riding home in a thunderstorm, Sarah fell asleep in her car seat behind me. In her parent's driveway, I sat and looked at her face for a long time. Who is this child? I wondered. I want to know her. Now that I am older and wiser and have the time and patience I didn't have as a father, I will approach Sarah as she approaches the pigeons—carefully, cautiously and quietly. And I will wonder as she does, how one can be so close and so forever far at the same time. She is not "mine" and she never will be. There are two people who think of her as "their" daughter. And there are four people who think of her as "their" granddaughter. But Sarah belongs only to herself. There will always be a moving space between us—this untraversable distance that must be treated with respect. And just as Sarah doesn't know what she would do if she ever actually caught a pigeon, I don't know what I'd do if I ever caught Sarah. To love something and to possess it are not the same thing. *(FRED exits.)*

(PIANO TRANSITION.)

"YES!"

JILL.

> IS THERE ANY FORCE OF NATURE HALF AS WILD
> AS THE INDEPENDENT SPIRIT OF A
>   FOUR-YEAR-OLD CHILD?—
> FEARLESS, TIRELESS, ABLE JUST TO BE,
> OVERFLOWING WITH CURIOSITY—
> THAT WAS ME BACK BEFORE DIET PILLS,
> DENTIST DRILLS,
> VISA® BILLS.
>
> THERE WAS A TIME WHEN YOU COULDN'T
>   HOLD ME BACK,
> WHEN MY IMAGINATION RAN RIOT;
> WHEN ME AND MY BROTHER FLEW TO MARS,
> AND COOKED CRAYONS IN THE TOASTER,
>   JUST TO TRY IT;
> THERE WAS A TIME WHEN WE MOONED
>   PASSING CARS,
> SHRIEKING WITH DEFIANT LAUGHTER;
> WHEN WE RODE ALL THE RIDES AND ATE ALL
>   THE JUNK AT THE FAIR,
> KNOWING WE'D REGRET IT SOON AFTER.
> THERE WAS A TIME WHEN I WOULD TRY
>   ANYTHING,
> WHEN I HAD CREATIVITY TO BURN.

**NOW IT SEEMS THE ONLY TIME I'M CREATIVE
IS WHEN I'M FILLING OUT MY TAX RETURN.**

(KATHLEEN, BRANISLAV and ED enter.)

BRANISLAV, ED, JILL KATHLEEN.
**IS THERE ANY FORCE OF NATURE MORE ALIVE
THAN A KID WITH AN IMAGINATION IN
OVER-DRIVE?—**

KATHLEEN.
BUILDING A SECRET CASTLE UNDER HER BED,

BRANISLAV.
ZOOMING AT THE SPEED OF LIGHT ON HIS SLED—

BRANISLAV, ED, JILL, KATHLEEN.
THAT WAS ME BACK BEFORE

KATHLEEN.
WRINKLE CREAMS,

ED.
INVESTMENT SCHEMES,

BRANISLAV, ED, JILL, KATHLEEN.
**FADING DREAMS
WHATEVER HAPPENED TO THE YES IN ME?**

KATHLEEN.
**EVER SINCE THE DAY I WAS BORN,
THE WORLD HAS SEEMED TO EDIT ME:**

GROWN-UPS SAID "STOP RUNNING THROUGH
    THE HOUSE;
WHY DON'T YOU SIT AND WATCH TV?"

ED.

AND "CAN'T YOU PICK SOME NICER FRIENDS?"

JILL.

AND "NO READING UNDER COVERS AFTER
    LIGHTS OUT."

BRANISLAV.

AND "DANCE CLASS IS FOR GIRLS."

ED.

AND "STOP CRYING OR I'LL GIVE YOU
    SOMETHING TO CRY ABOUT."

KATHLEEN.

MY FRIENDS SAID, "YOUR NEW LIPSTICK IS
    GROSS."

BRANISLAV.

AND "YOU REALLY LOOK LIKE A DORK WHEN
    YOU DANCE."

BRANISLAV, ED, JILL, KATHLEEN.

AND BIT BY BIT I'VE LOST THE YES,
THE WILLINGNESS TO TAKE A CHANCE.

KATHLEEN.

NOW I EDIT MYSELF: I SAY,

"WHAT DIFFERENCE COULD MY VOTE
POSSIBLY MAKE?"

JILL.
OR "THERE'S NOTHING I CAN DO FOR THE
HOMELESS."

ED.
OR "I DON'T HAVE THE TIME TO TAKE
ITALIAN LESSONS,

JILL.
OR WRITE MY MOM,

KATHLEEN.
OR LEARN TO PAINT,

BRANISLAV.
OR PLAY GUITAR,

ED.
OR PLANT A GARDEN."

JILL.
ALTHOUGH I SEEM TO FIND THE TIME TO
WATCH *ER*.

BRANISLAV, ED, JILL, KATHLEEN.
IS THERE ANY FORCE OF NATURE WITH MORE
POWER
THAN A KID SPINNING DAYDREAMS
AT A THOUSAND MILES AN HOUR?—

ED.
> **DIGGING FOR BURIED TREASURE IN THE
> BACKYARD,**

BRANISLAV.
> **HOLDING SECRET MEETINGS WITH THE DOG
> STANDING GUARD—**

BRANISLAV, ED, JILL, KATHLEEN.
> **THAT WAS ME BACK BEFORE**

BRANISLAV.
> **BOUNCING CHECKS,**

ED.
> **A SPITEFUL EX,**

KATHLEEN.
> **TEPID SEX.**

JILL.
> **IT'S NOT THAT I'D WANT TO BE A KID AGAIN—
> WETTING THE BED AND ALL OF THAT STUFF,**

BRANISLAV.
> **PLUS PIMPLES AND BRACES AND TEENAGE
> ANGST—
> THANKS ANYWAY, BUT ONCE WAS ENOUGH.**

ED.
> **BUT REALLY, ISN'T THERE SOME WAY
> TO KEEP MY CYNICISM AT BAY,**

BRANISLAV, ED, JILL, KATHLEEN.
> **TO LIVE A LITTLE CLOSER TO THE TRUTH,**
> **AS I DID SO SIMPLY IN MY YOUTH?**
>
> **YES I'D LOVE TO FIND THAT SPONTANEITY**
> **AS A GROWN-UP, IN MY WORK WITH MY**
> **FAMILY.**
> **IN THE MIDST OF DAILY ORDINARINESS,**
> **THERE HAS TO BE A GROWN-UP WAY TO SAY**
> **"YES."**

(They sit as in the opening scene, and all hands go up on the word "Yes." BRANISLAV, ED and KATHLEEN exit on applause. Note: If presenting the reduced-musical version—which eliminates the song "Yes!"—there is an optional intro to "The Briefcase" called "What Do You Do?—spoken version," found in Appendix E.)

THE BRIEFCASE

JILL. The most time-bound man I know lives in my neighborhood. He's always in a hurry—and always late. Always harassed and fuzzed out. I'm not exactly sure just what he does for a living, but it seems to involve buying and selling something downtown. He's a businessman.

His choice of appropriate transportation is a brand-new Range Rover®, a vehicle built by the British for high adventure in the wilds of Africa. It is equally capable in steep canyons, quicksand, and blizzard conditions. It can outrun a lion and take a rhino charge head-on. This particular "veldtmobile" is equipped with a winch, a gun rack and a CB radio, as well as an impressive stereo system, two cellular phones, a fax machine and a coffee maker in the glove compartment.

Daily, I see my neighbor rushing out of his house, burdened with the impediments of "high adventure." *(ED enters and mimes the action of the neighbor.)* Carrying golf bag, gym bag, lunch bag, raincoat, umbrella, coffee, a sack of garbage for the dumpster, and his briefcase.

About the briefcase. *(ED freezes.)* It is made of the purest, unblemished belting leather. The best part of the hides of four carefully selected cows, who gave their lives that he might carry this talisman of success. *(Carefully painting a detailed picture of excess.)* It has solid brass fittings, a combination lock, and his name embossed in gold.

So—it's a Tuesday morning around seven o'clock on a fine day in June.

(KATHLEEN enters, waves, ED maintains freeze.)

A neighbor lady and I hit the street headed for work about the same time. *(KATHLEEN freezes.)* She's a social worker for the Episcopal Church and drives an eight-year-old Ford "Just-Get-Me-There-And-Back-Please-God" sedan. And I drive a 1952 GMC "Go-Ahead-And-Hit-Me" pickup truck.

(KATHLEEN and ED break the freeze and begin to mime the following.) At the same time, the owner of the Range Rover® rushes up. His life is leveraged to the max these days, and his mind is in three continents at once. He is in no mood for small talk. He grunts at us as he loads his "lorry" for the "expedition" downtown,

into the front seat, and cranks the mighty engine like he's on the pole at the Indianapolis 500.

(With a strong sense of urgency, which continues throughout the chase scene, but does not speed up.) UH-OH! He's left his coffee cup and ... BRIEFCASE ... on the roof of the Range Rover® and there they remain as he rolls away.

TO THE RESCUE comes the nice lady social worker for the Episcopal Church in her Ford. She chases after him, urgently honking her horn, which he ignores because he is already on his cellular phone talking to London. But finally her unceasing ...

KATHLEEN. "HONK-HONK-HONK HONK-HONK-HONK HONK-HONK-HONK!"

JILL. ... gets the best of him. He throws the phone to the floor of the car, leans out the window, and displays the middle finger of his left hand. But the lady is *focused* on her rescue mission, and honks on while waving him to stop. I, in the meantime, driving close behind as a kind of "third float" in this little parade, likewise try to get his attention with my "aaooooogaah" horn I salvaged out of an old Model A. The combination of ...

KATHLEEN. "HONK-HONK-HONK!" *(Repeated ad lib.)*

JILL. and ... "AAAOOOGAAH-AAAOOOGAAH-AAAOOOGAAH!" *(Overlapping KATHLEEN, repeated ad lib.)* ... finally gets his attention. He *jams* on his brakes, *flings* open the door of the veldtmobile, and tries to get *out*—without first unlatching his seat belt. At the same moment, his morning cup of coffee *slides* off the roof, *bounces* across the hood, and *smashes* into the street. Followed by ... his BRASSBOUND BRIEFCASE ... which *crashes* onto the hood, *scrapes* across the paint with a fingernails-on-chalkboard screech, and *flops* into the street on top of the broken coffee cup. *(Pause. They are focused on the destroyed briefcase.)* The dear lady, mission accomplished, coasts slowly around the scene of the accident, smiles, waves at her neighbor dangling from the car in the clutches of his seat belt and sings out,

KATHLEEN. "Have a nice day!"

JILL. And no, she did not, as you might anticipate, run over the briefcase.

No, she did not.

I did.

The nice lady social worker and I meant well. It's not always easy doing good. When I told her later about running over the briefcase, she grinned. *(KATHLEEN smiles at JILL, then turns to the audience with a big grin.)* None of us is pure.

Did I run over it on purpose?

I don't know.

As I say, *none of us* is pure.

(Lights fade to transition as she exits, leaving the stage bare. PIANO TRANSITION.)

HOWARD

NARRATOR. NEXT. *(On a microphone, over the sound system. Not visible. A light focuses on a trapdoor in the floor. BRANISLAV lifts the lid a few inches with his head, and peers out. He drops down again, disappearing for a moment, pause.)* NEXT.

(BRANISLAV emerges once more, this time climbing halfway out. He is holding a piece of paper. If a trap is not available, the actor should enter as though he has just climbed a long distance to get there. The implication, without being overly literal, is that he is at the gates of heaven and must pass this interrogation before he will be allowed entry.)

Have you completed the form?

BRANISLAV. Where am I?

NARRATOR. Have you completed the form?

BRANISLAV. It sure was a long climb up.

NARRATOR. Yes. Have you completed the form?

BRANISLAV. Almost.

NARRATOR. Almost?

BRANISLAV. I...uh...just have one question.

NARRATOR. A question?

BRANISLAV. Yeah.

NARRATOR. Well?

BRANISLAV. About this one blank.

NARRATOR. Which blank?

BRANISLAV. The one that says "Religion:_____."

NARRATOR. Yes? *(BRANISLAV shrugs his shoulders questioningly and looks expectantly into the darkness of the theatre.)* Do you believe in God? *(A pause.)* Do you believe in God?

BRANISLAV *(a nervous pause. He decides to answer indirectly).* I believe in Howard.

NARRATOR. Howard? You believe in Howard?

BRANISLAV. It all has to do with my mother's maiden name.

NARRATOR. Your mother's maiden name.

BRANISLAV. Was Howard. And she was part of a big family in Memphis, "The Howard Family." And so I grew up
thinking of myself as a member of the Howard family.

NARRATOR. So what does that have to do with God?

BRANISLAV (*emerging from the trap and sitting on the
rim, or stepping onto the stage*). Oh, well, it's really
quite simple. See, what happened was that I got packed
off to Sunday School at around age four, and the first
thing I learned was the Lord's Prayer, which begins
"Our Father which art in heaven, Hallowed be Thy
name." And what I heard was "Our Father, which art in
heaven, HOWARD be thy name." And since little kids
tend to mutter their prayers anyway, nobody realized
what I was saying, so I went right on believing that
God's name was Howard. And that I was a member of
His family—the Howards. Since I was also told that my
grandfather had died and gone to heaven, God and my
grandfather got all mixed up in my mind as one and the
same. Which meant that I had a pretty comfy notion
about God. When I knelt beside my bed each night and
prayed, "Our Father, which art in heaven, Howard be
thy name," I thought about my grandfather and what a
big shot he was. Because, of course, the prayer ends
with "For Thine is the kingdom, and the power, and the
glory *forever and ever!* Amen." I went to bed feeling
pretty well connected to the universe for a long time.

NARRATOR (*after a pause*). You're putting me on, right?

BRANISLAV. No, no, not at all. *I belonged to the whole
big scheme of things.* I lived and worked and had my
being in the family store. The whole universe was a
Howard Family enterprise.

NARRATOR. So. Do you still believe in...Howard?

BRANISLAV *(hesitates, then decides to answer the question honestly. He discreetly closes the trap to avoid being thrown back down, in the event they don't like his answer).* Let me put it this way; the thirteenth-century Christian mystic, Meister Eckhart, said, "The eye with which *I* see God is the same eye with which *God* sees *me*."

NARRATOR *(at his wit's end).* What the hell is that supposed to mean?

BRANISLAV. Not only do I believe in Howard, but Howard ... believes in me.

(BLACKOUT. PIANO TRANSITION.)

CHRISTMAS/VALENTINE'S DAY

(ED and JILL bring on three chairs and set up a waiting room. ED stands behind his chair. JILL exits. During this transition, KATHLEEN enters as an old woman escorting FRED as an old man. They are wearing winter scarves and coats. They sit.)

ED. It's February and I have an appointment for a physical. In the waiting room are two other people much older than I—very nice looking, tidy, intelligent-looking couple, both probably in their eighties. Here to see the doctor, too, I guess. *(He sits, and begins reading a magazine.)* So I'm sitting there in my February state of mind and this nice old man next to me nudges me and says ...

FRED. "Hey ... Merry Christmas."

ED *(to audience).* This is February, right? Yeah, it's February. And I look at him. "Merry Christmas to you." And he sits back *(FRED starts singing.)* and he starts singing...

FRED. "Oh, you better watch out, you better not cry, You better not pout, I'm telling you why, Santa Claus is coming to town."

ED *(overlapping the end of FRED's song).* ...all the way through, finishes the song, says...

FRED. "Hey...Merry Christmas!"

ED. And I say "Merry Christmas" back to him, and I'm thinking... "Could be me." *(Indicating "maybe I'm the one who's crazy.")*

(JILL enters as the nurse.)

ED. Well, the nurse comes for him and he goes off. *(FRED exits with JILL.)*

KATHLEEN *(sees ED's eyes roll, and feels compelled to enlighten him).* We've been married for sixty years, and Fred's eighty-seven now, and, well, in our family we say his wiring is coming loose. He's had a few little strokes, and there's some Alzheimer's. He's just getting old, and every once in a while, he suddenly announces it's Christmas.

The first time he did it, I thought *I* was crazy. I thought, this is the stupidest thing I've ever heard, because he shouted from upstairs "Hey! It's Christmas Eve! Merry Christmas! Let's decorate the tree!" It was so strange. *(Very concerned.)* I called my daughters and I told them what was going on. Well, they came over. *(Dumbfounded.)* And they brought some presents, too. They said, "For God's sake, Mother, it's not illegal." Well, we had a wonderful time.

And the best part of that whole affair was that he said to me, "You know, I can't remember some of the things when I was a child. Tell me about Christmas when I was a little boy."

Well, he had a terrible childhood. His mother was a drunk. His father ran off. He was virtually orphaned and had to leave home when he was very, very young. I didn't want to tell him about that. So I did something I have never, ever done or thought I would do in sixty years with this man.

I lied to him.

(Getting caught up in the memory.) I told him about the Christmas he got a rocking horse. And I told him about the Christmas he got a bicycle and the Christmas he was in the pageant. *(Remembering the look on his face.)* Oh, and he loved it. And we had a wonderful time. One of the best Christmases we ever had, even if it was July.

And the strange thing, along about bedtime that day he forgot all about it. It went out of his mind and we never did get to Christmas. Christmas Eve and good memories seemed to be enough.

But four months later it happened all over again. I heard him singing carols upstairs one morning, and here came Christmas down the stairs. MERRY CHRISTMAS! *(Momentarily caught up in her memory of this painfully difficult moment of letting go.)* And I thought ...

what harm?

(Regaining her composure.) So this has happened four or five times now. In July. And in October ... twice in December. And now in February.

Every time, he wants me to tell him about his childhood again and I do. I'm getting so good at lying about how wonderful his Christmas used to be that I half believe it myself. I call the girls each time—just say "Merry Christmas" into the phone—and here they come. They always bring him presents and sing carols and bake cookies—the whole thing. And twice we've even got as far as putting up a tree. They *love* to do it. (*We hear FRED and JILL singing.*)

ED. Just then old Fred comes shuffling back up the hall with the nurse.

(*FRED and JILL enter, singing the final line of "Jingle Bells."*)

FRED & JILL. "Oh what fun it is to ride in a one horse open sleigh." (*FRED steps to ED.*)

FRED (*warmly to ED, as if seeing him for the first time*). Hey ... Merry Christmas.

ED (*completely won over, and deeply touched by the sweetness of the moment, responds to FRED*). Merry Christmas. (*FRED crosses with JILL towards the exit.*)

KATHLEEN (*gathering her purse*). See, the girls don't think of it as Christmas anymore...they think of it as Father's Day. (*She looks back at FRED.*) And I kind of think of it as Valentine's Day. (*PIANO TRANSITION: "Jingle Bells." She crosses to FRED. Turns back to ED.*)

Merry Christmas.

(*She leads FRED off as ED watches.*)

GEEK DANCING

(BRANISLAV brings on a small cafe table and places it as if at the side of a dance floor. He and JILL place two chairs at the table. JILL sits. This is completed on the final chord of the transition music.)

BRANISLAV *(to audience)*. Do you know about geek dancing? *(Pause.)* Yeah, you heard right. Not Greek dancing but GEEK dancing. *(He sits.)* Actually GEEK is in the dictionary. It refers to a carnival performer whose act consists of doing weird things... like biting the head off a live chicken.

JILL *(to audience)*. In current slang, a geek is someone who *looks* like he might be capable of doing something like that. A person who bears watching.

(FRED enters. He is wearing, or carrying, his hat and coat from the preceding scene, but is not playing the old man from the doctor's office.)

BRANISLAV. But, I've also heard kids using the word geek to describe anybody who is *older...* *(A friendly dig at FRED.)* and "independent" in lifestyle.

FRED. I think there's a kind of compliment in there somewhere. It means a little strange, but interesting. *(Removing coat and hat.)* I guess that's true. A lot of us older types are a bit "geeky." You reach the point in life when you just decide to go ahead and "weird out." You start out the door in your bedroom slippers, headed for the grocery store... you don't go back and change into shoes. To hell with it. Or you go out to the mailbox in your bathrobe—your oldest, sleaziest bathrobe... and you don't give a damn who sees you. Or the doorbell rings... you don't check the mirror to see what you look like. You just open the door. It's their problem, whoever they are. Some people call this "going to seed." Others call it "the beginning of wisdom." Take your pick. *(BRANISLAV rises to make room for FRED at table. FRED sits.)* Anyway, about geek dancing.

BRANISLAV. When I am in the need for an uplifting experience, I go where people dance. I don't mean to joints where people go to get crocked and then wobble around the floor to music. *(Stepping onto the dance floor.)* I mean places where people who really like to dance *(Does a little flourish to demonstrate.)* ... go.

JILL. I like dancers. I've never met a serious dancer who wasn't a pretty fine human being. And I enjoy being surprised by just who the dancers are. I love seeing the most unlikely couples get up on the floor and waltz like angels. *(PIANO MUSIC: Vamp begins. Lights shift towards mood lighting.)*

FRED. My favorite place, the Uptown Tavern, has traditional jazz on Sunday nights from 6:30 to 9:30. The geek band plays swing music from Chicago and New York. *(There is a jazz lick from the piano.)*

BRANISLAV. I like to look around and find the king-hill champion geek for the evening. An old guy, balding, white hair, kinda short. The kind who sort of lists to port when he walks. One who you might think was strictly nursing-home material if you saw him at a bus stop. But you see him here. And you know. A dancer.

JILL. And he usually has his wife with him... the "Geekess." A bit younger, always fluffed up a bit for dancing and has been for fifty years. Check her shoes. If they are black with mid-heels and a strap across the instep, it's a sure bet what she came here for, and what she is going to do.

BRANISLAV. Well, the music cranks up. *(FRED now assumes the character of the old Geek. He limps onto the dance floor with the invisible Geekess holding his hand. JILL and BRANISLAV look on.)* He takes her by the hand and kind of limps onto the floor. *(Music stops.)* It's an act, just to set you up. And then, it happens. *(Mirrorball effect begins. PIANO kicks into the melody of "You Made Me Love You.")*

JILL *(while FRED pantomimes the following).* She steps into a permanent spotlight formed by his embrace, the years fall away, and once again Cinderella and the Prince move to the music in the room and the music in their hearts.

BRANISLAV. He dances flatfooted and with an economy of motion.

JILL. She responds to unseen suggestions to twirl out—and around—and back. It takes about forty years to dance with a partner this way.

BRANISLAV. Their eyes meet from time to time. *(BRANISLAV mirrors FRED as he dips his partner.)* You have to love someone a long time to do what they're doing. *(They rise from the dip.)* I *want* to be, and fully *intend* to be, an *old geek dancer.*

FRED. Ah, then you'll be needing the best Geek trainer available.

(KATHLEEN enters as the old lady from the doctor's office. Dances with BRANISLAV.)

FRED. It is a public responsibility for us Geeks to help everybody stay young as long as they can, to set a good example for the next generation of Geeks. And I don't want to die quietly in my bed either...but at the end of the last dance some lovely night, sit down in a chair, smile, and pass on. *(FRED cuts in on BRANISLAV, and dances with KATHLEEN.)*

JILL. All this reminds me of something I heard about the Hopi Indians. They don't think there is much difference between dancing...and praying. And that both are necessary for a long life. The Hopis should know, I guess; they have been through a lot and they're still around. *(FRED and KATHLEEN momentarily stop dancing to listen.)* They say that to be a useful Hopi...is to be one who has a quiet heart...and takes part in *all* the dances.

BRANISLAV *(raising his hand).* Yes!

(PIANO MUSIC: There is a sweeping glissando back to "You Made Me Love You." FRED removes KATHLEEN's coat on the glissando, revealing a lovely dancing dress. He tosses the coat to BRANISLAV who then puts it on JILL. As KATHLEEN and FRED sweep around the dance floor, BRANISLAV puts on FRED's coat and hat, and the young couple, now honorary Geeks, join FRED and KATHLEEN dancing. Near the end of the dance, ED enters with a blanket that he is twirling as a dance partner. He takes C on the final note, dipping his blanket-partner while the other two couples pose R and L. The two couples exit on applause.)

"A TOMB WITH A VIEW"
(The Song)

ED *(slings blanket over one shoulder).*

> **A WHILE BACK I THOUGHT**
> **I'D BUY A CEMETERY PLOT.**

(Spoken.) What an odd shopping experience.

> **THE MOST IMPORTANT THING IN THE**
> **EVALUATION**
> **OF REAL ESTATE IS LOCATION, LOCATION,**
> **LOCATION.**
> **BUT I THOUGHT "IT'S A GRAVE; WHO CARES**
> **ABOUT THE VIEW?"**
> **RESALE VALUE SEEMS PRETTY TRIVIAL, TOO.**

(Suggests arriving at the gravesite.)

> **WELL, I BOUGHT MY PLOT;**
> **AND NOW I VISIT THE SPOT**
> **FROM TIME TO TIME,**
> **WHEN I FEEL THAT I'M**
> **GETTING TOO CAUGHT UP IN THE OLD RAT**
> **RACE.**
> **PAYING MY RESPECTS AT MY FINAL RESTING**
> **PLACE**
> **ALWAYS UNTWISTS THE SNARLS IN MY SOUL**
> **AND MIND,**
> **WHEN I FORGET WHAT'S IMPORTANT AMIDST**
> **THE DAILY GRIND.**
> **RECENTLY I NOTICED TWO GRAVE STONES**
> **PRESENT**
> **NEAR MY OWN, MARKED**

(Indicating each grave.)

> **"GRIMM" AND "PLEASANT."**

BEING BURIED BETWEEN "GRIMM" AND
   "PLEASANT" HAS A CERTAIN CACHET—
WOULDN'T YOU SAY? *(LIGHTS: night effect.)*

ONCE LATE AT NIGHT,
I WALKED TO THE SITE, *(Spreads out blanket C.)*
BRINGING MY FAVORITE BLANKET ALONG
   WITH ME. *(Lies down.)*
I STRETCHED OUT ON MY GRAVE, AND MADE
   A STARTLING DISCOVERY:

(LIGHTS: Stars appear.)

(Spoken.) This grave has an incredible view! Looking
straight up! *(Gradually rising.)*

STARLIGHT HAD COME MILLIONS OF
   LIGHT-YEARS FOR ME TO SEE.
I WAS STRUCK BY THE HEAVENS' MAGNITUDE
   AND COMPLEXITY—
AND I REALIZED—I'M A PART OF THAT
   GEOMETRY.

(Crossing D.)

I'VE NEVER LIKED THE VERSE THAT SAID,
"DUST THOU ART—TO DUST THOU SHALT
   RETURN."
WE ARE ENERGY,
INTERCHANGEABLE WITH LIGHT—HUMANITY
IS DREAMS, HOPES AND FEARS, BLISS AND
   MELANCHOLY,
HELD TOGETHER BY WISDOM, PULLED APART
   BY FOLLY.

(Spoken.) So much more than dust!

THE BIBLE VERSE SHOULD SAY INSTEAD,
"MIRACLE THOU ART AND TO MYSTERY
   THOU SHALT RETURN."

(Returning to the blanket, remaining standing.)
    **THE LIGHT FROM THESE STARS, THIS LIGHT
    THAT I'M SEEING,
    STARTED TOWARD ME BEFORE I CAME INTO
    BEING.
    THE STARS MAY HAVE DIED OUT, LONG
    BEFORE THIS NIGHT.**
(Spoken.) That's a scientific fact.
    **MY LIFE GIVES OFF ANOTHER KIND OF LIGHT.
    THAT LIGHT MAY SHINE ON AND ON,
    LONG AFTER THE SOURCE IS GONE.**

(The other four actors enter during the final PIANO MUSIC as if stepping outdoors on a beautiful starry night to gaze up at the stars. They are all lost in thought.)

A TOMB WITH A VIEW
(Alternate Spoken Version)

ED *(slings blanket over one shoulder).* A while back, I decided it was time to buy a cemetery plot. What an odd shopping experience. Popular wisdom says, the three most important things to consider in real estate decisions are: location, location, location! But I thought: "It's a grave ... what difference does a *view* really make?" And resale value? Not a problem.

    Well, I made my purchase, and now, from time to time, I like to go pay my respects at my final resting place. *(Suggests arriving at the gravesite.)* Visiting my own grave always helps untwist the snarls in my mind and soul, especially when I lose track of what's important. On a recent visit, I noticed that the neighboring "property owners" were James and Edith Grimm, and Jacob Pleasant. *(Indicating each grave.)* Being buried between "Grimm" and "Pleasant" has a poetic rightness about it, don't you think? *(LIGHTS: Night effect.)*

Once I went up to the cemetery late at night, bringing my favorite blanket with me. *(Spreads the blanket and stretches out.)* I laid it down on my grave, stretched out, and was STARTLED! ... *(LIGHTS: Stars appear.)* This grave has an incredible view! Looking straight up! I could see starshine that was coming to me from millions of light-years away.

(Filled with wonder.) Trying to conceive of the magnitude and complexity of space, I just laid there, looking into the infinite darkness, filled with all that *light.*

(Rising to one knee.) You know, I have never liked the verse that says "Dust thou art and to dust thou shalt return." We are energy, which is interchangeable with *light.* We are fire and water and earth. We are also dreams, hopes and fears, held together by wisdom, and pulled apart by folly. So much more than dust. *(Standing.)* The Bible verse should say instead: "Miracle thou art, and to mystery thou shalt return." *(PIANO MUSIC.)*

The light I see from my grave *(Indicating the stars.)* started traveling through space ages before I came into being. The stars, which are the source of that light, may have actually died out by now. Gone. That is a scientific fact. But somehow, the light still shines on.

My life gives off another kind of light. That light *(Indicating himself.)* may shine on—long after the source is gone. *(Indicating his grave. He stands gazing up at the sky in awe.)*

(The other four actors enter during the final PIANO MUSIC as if stepping outdoors on a beautiful starry night to gaze up at the stars. They are all lost in thought.)

ARE THERE ANY QUESTIONS?

(Breaking the reverie of the stargazing moment, the voice of the narrator is heard over the sound system. He is not visible to the actors.)

NARRATOR. Are there any questions? *(Pause.)* ... Are there any questions?

JILL. What is the meaning of life?

NARRATOR. I beg your pardon?

JILL. What is the meaning of life?

NARRATOR. Are you kidding me?

JILL. Well, who knows, you may have the answer, and I'd really hate to miss it because I was too socially inhibited to ask. *(Lights shift.)*

BRANISLAV. Once,

FRED. and only once,

JILL. I asked that question:

ED. "What is the meaning of life?"

BRANISLAV. "What is the meaning of life?"

KATHLEEN. "What is the meaning of life?"

FRED. "What is the meaning of life?"

JILL. ...and got a serious answer. An answer that is still with me. The place where this happened has a distinct power of its own. *(PIANO MUSIC. They settle in, sitting on chairs or levels, and begin telling the story.)* On the

Greek island of Crete, near a small village on a rocky bay, sits an institute dedicated to human understanding and peace, but especially to reconciliation between Germans and the natives of Crete.

KATHLEEN. The site is important because it overlooks a small airstrip where Nazi paratroopers invaded the island and were attacked by peasants wielding kitchen knives and hay scythes.

FRED. The retribution was terrible. Populations of whole villages were lined up and shot for assaulting Hitler's finest troops.

ED (*stepping D, and indicating the two burial sights. The others follow his gaze*). High above the institute is a cemetery with a single cross, marking the mass grave of the native partisans. And across the bay on another hill is the regimented burial ground of the Nazi paratroopers. The memorials are placed so that all might see and never forget.

KATHLEEN. Hatred was the only weapon the Greeks had left at the end, and it was the weapon many vowed never to give up.

JILL. In this historical place, where the stone of hatred is hard and thick, the existence of an institute devoted to healing the wounds of war is a fragile paradox.

ED (*returning to his seat*). So how has it come to be here?

FRED. The answer is a man. Alexander Papaderos (*Pronounced Pah-pah-deh-ros*), doctor of philosophy, teacher, politician, son of this soil. At the end of the war, Papaderos came to believe that the people of Crete and those of Germany had much to learn from each other, much to give one another. For if they could forgive, and construct a creative relationship, then any people on this earth could.

(JILL speaks DR or DC, KATHLEEN, ED, and BRANIS-LAV transform the space into a classroom at the institute by arranging the five chairs on a diagonal facing UL. The [optional] window flies in UL, marking the front of the classroom. KATHLEEN, BRANISLAV and ED sit facing the window. FRED has remained standing DL at the back of the classroom configuration.)

JILL. Well, Papaderos succeeded. The institute became a reality—a conference ground on the site of horror, and a source of productive interaction between the two countries. By the time I came to the institute for summer session, Alexander Papaderos was already a living legend. One look at him and you saw his strength, his intelligence and his passion. *(She sits.)*

FRED. At the end of the last session of a two-week seminar, Papaderos rose from his chair in the back of the room and walked to the front, *(He crosses U to the window.)* where he stood in the bright Greek sunlight of an open window and looked out. *(He becomes Papaderos, but because of the fractured storytelling that follows, he does not speak with a dialect.)*

JILL. We followed his gaze across the bay to the iron cross marking the German cemetery. He turned and asked:

FRED. "Are there any questions?"

BRANISLAV *(after a pause, turning to the audience).* Quiet quilted the room. These two weeks had generated enough questions for a lifetime, but for now, there was only silence.

JILL. So, I asked. *(She stands, raising her hand.)* "Doctor Papaderos, what is the meaning of life?" *(She remains focused on FRED as Papaderos.)*

ED *(KATHLEEN, BRANISLAV and ED chuckle and stir. They rise and start to go)*. People laughed at the absurdity of the question, and they stirred to go.

BRANISLAV. He raised his hand and stilled the room. *(ED and BRANISLAV sit, KATHLEEN sits or remains off to the side.)*

FRED *(locks eyes with JILL, and seeing that she is serious, he decides to answer)*. "I will answer the question." *(He pulls out a small round mirror from his pocket.)*

JILL. He fished into his leather billfold and pulled out a very small round mirror, *(PIANO FLOURISH as he holds up the mirror.)* ...and what he said went like this:

(JILL and FRED freeze looking at each other. One by one, the other three step out, taking a part of his story, and personalizing it.)

KATHLEEN *(stepping D)*. "When I was a small child, during the war, we were very, very poor and lived in a remote village. One day, on the road, I came across the pieces of a broken mirror." *(She suggests picking up a piece, and reveals a mirror identical to FRED's.)* "A German motorcycle had been wrecked in this place."

BRANISLAV *(rises, stepping D of chairs)*. "I tried to find all the pieces and fit them together, but it was not possible, so I kept only the largest piece. This one." *(Revealing an identical mirror.)* "And, by scratching it on a stone, I made it round." *(PIANO MUSIC. He crosses as he demonstrates the game.)* "I began to play with it as a toy, and became fascinated by the fact that I could reflect light into dark places—into deep holes and crevices and dark closets. It became a game for me to try to get light into the most inaccessible places I could find." *(He stops reflecting the light and focuses on one spot.)*

ED *(rising, he steps D revealing an identical mirror)*. "I kept the little mirror, and as I went about my growing up, I would take it out in idle moments and renew the challenge of the game. But as I became an adult, I realized that this was more than just a game, but a metaphor for what I might do with my life. I came to understand that I am not the light, or the source of the light. But the light—

BRANISLAV. Truth,

KATHLEEN. Understanding,

FRED. Knowledge—

ED. —is there, and it will shine in dark places only if I reflect it." *(KATHLEEN, ED, and BRANISLAV subtly begin reflecting the light onto faces in the audience.)*

FRED *(they have created a stage picture which now places FRED at the strongest focal point. He speaks to JILL and audience)*. "I am a fragment of a mirror whose whole design and shape I do not know. Nevertheless, with what I have, I can reflect light into the dark places of this world—into the black places in the hearts of men—and change some things in some people. Perhaps others may see and do likewise. This is what I am about. This is the meaning of *my* life." *(He begins reflecting the light onto JILL's face.)*

JILL. And then he took the small mirror, and holding it carefully, *(PIANO MUSIC.)* caught the bright rays of daylight streaming through the window, and reflected them onto my face, and onto my hands, folded on the

classroom desk. *(Taking out a mirror exactly like the others, she begins to shine it in the audience.)*
ED *(stepping D)*. Are there any questions?
KATHLEEN *(stepping D)*. Are there any questions?
BRANISLAV *(stepping D)*. Are there any questions?
JILL *(stepping D)*. Are there any questions?
FRED *(stepping D)*. Are there any questions?

(LIGHTS fade with a long delay on the mirror ball [not turning] revealing hundreds of tiny reflected points of light. Effect can fade to black as an optional ending of Act Two, or a special comes up on JILL for the reprise of "Reflect The Light.")

"REFLECT THE LIGHT" *(Reprise)*

JILL.

> THERE'S NO WAY TO MEASURE
>   WHAT THESE FRAGMENTS ARE WORTH—
> SCATTERED MOMENTS OF CONNECTION
>   TO LIFE ON THIS EARTH;
> FLASHES OF UNDERSTANDING,
>   THAT CAN SET YOUR SOUL ABLAZE
> AND FLICKER SOFTLY
>   THROUGH ALL OF YOUR DAYS.

ALL.

> STOP NOW AND LISTEN.
>   CAN YOU HEAR A FAINT MELODY?
> JUST OUTSIDE HERE, ALL AROUND US—
>   A GREAT SYMPHONY.

BRANISLAV.	ALL.
BUT NOTHING IN LIFE	OOH
HAS THE POWER TO INSPIRE	
LIKE ADDING YOUR OWN VOICE	AHH
TO THE MIGHTY CHOIR.	

ALL.

HOW CAN WE LIVE IN THE DARK,
WHEN WE COULD BE PART OF THAT LIGHT?
HOW DO WE CAPTURE THAT SPARK
AND REFLECT IT INTO THE HEART OF THE
    NIGHT?

THE END
CURTAIN CALL

APPENDIX A
Production Notes

All I Really Need to Know I Learned in Kindergarten was a short essay written by an interesting man in Seattle. It found its way onto bulletin boards and refrigerators, reminding thousands of people of the simple truths that are the foundation of our lives. It is now several years later, and that list of simple truths has traveled around the world reaching millions of people, and has even been entered into our congressional record. And the simple truths still apply.

Robert Fulghum has been on a fantastical journey that made him one of the world's most popular writers in the latter part of the twentieth century. And now we have had the privilege of tagging along for part of that journey with this stage adaptation of his work. Like so many readers, we were struck by the profound insight and charming wit of this wonderful storyteller. So we thought, why not try to translate it into our own language of the theatre? And what a joy it has been to see these great stories come to life for thousands of audience members around the world...turning what was a solo reading-chair experience into that amazing communal celebration that can only take place in the theatre.

Now, we hope to share some of what we have learned on our journey with *Kindergarten*. Because it started out in literary form, it required the contributions of actors, directors, music directors and designers to transform it into theatre. Taking what appears to be simple and giving it the substance and shape required to engage an audience is somewhat tricky, but very satisfying and great fun.

The show was developed in front of audiences across the United States and overseas—in major commercial venues, LORT theatres, community theatres and high schools. These notes (as well as the stage directions in the script) are gathered from *all* these experiences, and will hopefully be useful to you as you apply your own creativity to the material.

In translating Robert Fulghum's unique style, one of the most important things we discovered was to keep it simple, to make theatrical choices that would enhance the art of storytelling. The depth and complexity of the show is found in the words.

So now we welcome you to the journey, and in the spirit of George Bernard Shaw, Eugene O'Neill and other playwrights known for their long-winded notes and stage directions, we offer you "all we ever learned" about *All I Really Need to Know I Learned in Kindergarten.*

Ernest Zulia and David Caldwell

AT THE HEART OF THIS PIECE

Bill Cosby once said the key to telling a good story was to walk onstage knowing he had a wonderful secret to reveal. His demeanor said, in effect, "Trust me, I'm headed towards a destination that will be worth the ride; be prepared for colorful stops and details along the way." This involves a certain amount of teasing as he unfolds a story. At the heart of each story in this show is the storyteller's desire to share a moment of enlightenment. Sometimes it is a profound personal revelation, a glimpse of truth. Other times it is an interesting observation that enriches his or her appreciation of life. And it all adds up to a greater story. In preparing the material, it helps to start backwards. When your emotional, intellectual, and spiritual destination is clear, you will be in a stronger position to craft the moments leading up to that destination. However, beware of playing the end at the beginning. Too much reverence for the "message" when you are just starting out can kill the payoff. It is often only near the end, when the actor lays down the mantle of storyteller and addresses the audience as an equal, that the strongest human connection is made. The moment is not about the storyteller overindulging in feelings evoked by a memory, but rather, about genuinely sharing something significant.

The show is a comedy. And nothing opens the heart and mind like laughter. The laughter in this material often lowers the audience's guard, allowing the truth and drama within each piece to resonate deeply.

It is the storytellers' sense of humor, together with some humility and an awareness of their own foibles, that keeps them from seeming pious or pretentious. Their maturity and intelligence give depth to the material and keep it from becoming cute. These are people who are able to catch glimpses of "the fragments of light" just under the surface of everyday life.

If the material is viewed only from the surface, it can appear simplistic and pat. The substance and dramatic conflict emerge as the stories are examined more deeply. The questioning mind of the storyteller carries him or her through a struggle of sorts. This is the key to the dramatic conflict which brings theatrical life to the stories.

The material is optimistic, but the storytellers are not a group of Pollyannas. It may be helpful to know that the author's point of view comes from rich and varied life experiences. As a Unitarian minister, he has married people, buried people, and walked with many through difficult personal and family struggles. As a high-school art and philosophy teacher, he has explored issues of imagination and creativity and how they apply to our perceptions of life.

His extensive travels have taken him around the world more than once exploring the ways and beliefs of different cultures.

Throughout his writing he shares insight on matters of depression, adoption, suicide, and divorce, all of which have touched his personal life in one way or another. He takes great joy in music and art, but nothing seems to make him happier than genuine laughter. He can be quite irreverent and laughs at himself a lot, helping to make him a master of the comic observation.

Fulghum often says this material does not teach anything we don't already know, but hopefully it reflects a little light onto what is already inside us all.

The word "Yes" runs throughout the show, and the cast spends two hours telling stories about the "Yes" of life...the things that give life meaning...the things that turn our lives into more than just a series of events. And "Yes" can be discovered through our ability to "LOOK."

STRUCTURE AND SEQUENCE

There is an emotional arc with dramatic and comic beats strategically placed to give theatrical structure and form to the evening. It is sometimes difficult to sense this while reading the script or during the rehearsal process. The links between pieces may not always be obvious, but they have proven to be quite effective. Act One introduces the author's voice and philosophical point of view, as well as the personalities of the performers. This structure is based on a flow of ideas and moods, and the progression is emotional. Act Two travels the journey of marriage, family, career, faith, old age and death.

It is possible to mix and match stories from the script and the appendix creating a version of *Kindergarten* that suits your specific organization, event and audience, but please proceed with caution. Every sequence generates a specific rhythm. Stories must be organized with enough variety to sustain the interest of the audience. This requires a carefully orchestrated rhythm that does not focus on the affection one might have for individual stories, but instead focuses on each act as a whole. The recommended sequences in this script were created taking all these things into account.

The transitions between scenes contribute greatly to the momentum and overall impact of each act. It is helpful if they are tightly choreographed to allow the story that is ending to resonate just long enough before we are launched into the next story. Some pieces obviously require more time to ponder than others. The piano transitions have been written very specifically to bridge the stories well. If they have to be lengthened to accommodate a slow scene change, these delicate emotional links could lose their effectiveness, causing the show to drag.

THE TEXT

The vast majority of the words spoken in this script are taken directly from the texts of Robert Fulghum. They have been carefully edited and sometimes rearranged to make them more stageworthy. In some instances, we have deliberately kept the literary flavor of the language to provide variety, texture, and a poetic lyricism.

Referring back to the original stories and others from the five books is useful as background information.

We have attempted to lay out the text on the page in a way that suggests the architecture of each piece. Each paragraph or separate line can be thought of as a building block in the story. The transitions between these blocks are often as important as the blocks themselves. If the performer takes the time to make the emotional or intellectual transition from one image or idea to the next, then the audience will also make the transition. This contributes greatly to the build and overall impact of the story.

SOME TIPS ON THE PERFORMANCE STYLE

Storytelling is a very intimate performance style. It is much like a conversation with the audience. The approach is fairly obvious in the solo pieces, which allow the performer to step in and out of the action of the stories, commenting along the way. In the ensemble pieces, such as "Cinderella" and "Are There Any Questions?" we have noticed that actors often instinctively deliver narration to one another as if they were speaking dialogue in a play behind the fourth wall. In the show's presentational style, it is more effective for the actors to speak primarily to the audience while occasionally including the others onstage.

Although the cast is likely to be made up of extremely different individuals, a very tightly knit ensemble helps in delivering this material. Because they are called upon to speak with one voice, the storytellers have to be keenly in tune with each other and listen to every word spoken. Each helps build the ensemble stories to a climax, and the audience can get lost along the way if one person is out of step. They all contribute to the momentum of a piece, helping to infuse it with energy. But it is not simply a matter of cue pick-ups, because there is often a reaction time to many lines that must be taken into account before delivering the next piece of the story. They must each own the other's lines as if they were their own. It's as if they were all hosts of the same party, with the audience as the guests.

Since the actors deliver most of the lines directly to the audience, they will discover many of the nuances of the material only when they can play it off living, breathing, laughing bodies. As a result, there is a unique rehearsal problem, because the actors' scene partner is often the audience. For this reason, it can be very useful to invite friends and staff in for some rehearsals to give the actors someone to play off of while making acting choices. More so than with other shows, we have found that large crowds bring totally new reactions and are much more vocal than a small handful of people.

In certain stories, a fourth wall does exist for specific characters, creating more traditional scenes (e.g., Sigmund Wollman and the young college student in "Problems and Inconveniences," the older couple in "Christmas/Valentine's Day," and Norman and the kindergarten teacher in "Cinderella"). These characters exist only in the world of the story and do not relate to the audience. The narrator, however, exists in both the world of the story and in the world of the audience, providing the link which keeps these pieces in the presentational storytelling-style of the rest of the show. The actors should be aware when they are stepping into a story and reliving the experience, and when they are stepping out of a story and commenting on what has just happened.

The audience creates much of each story in their imaginations. A slower pace than you might expect is often required to allow them to complete the images, and digest the ideas. The storytellers are guides, and if the words come too fast, the world of the story cannot flower. It is as if they are describing a movie, one frame at a time.

The rhythms of the language in this script are not conducive to ad-libbing between actor and audience. When the voice and structure of a story is interrupted by unscripted banter, the story loses its direction and momentum.

It is useful to provide carefully choreographed focus for the audience, especially in the ensemble pieces. As a rule of thumb, the narrators should watch whomever is speaking. Also, when something in the text is being acted out by characters, it is essential that the narrator acknowledge the action and refer to it during his or her narration. Likewise, when introducing or discussing characters, the narrator should refer to them while speaking. This will help avoid the confusion caused by split focus.

One final tip. There is a significant difference between acting and storytelling. While presenting a character in a play, the actor must create the illusion that he or she does not know what is coming next—the illusion of spontaneity. While telling a story, the storyteller knows exactly what is coming next and uses the illusion of spontaneity as a device to enhance the story.

EXERCISE

Because the show is so segmented, we found it necessary to create an exercise that would allow everyone a comprehensive connection to all the material. For example, even though one person performs "The Bench," it is important that everyone in the show has an understanding of it, because it is central to the show's philosophy.

It is basically a "round-robin" exercise. The actors and director sit around the table and read the script aloud to each other. Moving clockwise, each actor reads one paragraph or line. Then the next actor reads the next paragraph or line. This includes monologues as well as ensemble pieces. It works even better if actors do not end up reading their own lines.

In the end, the entire cast has a stronger awareness of the voice of the author and a deeper connection to the entire show. Plus, it's a fun exercise for everyone.

ABOUT THE SET

The show can easily be performed on a flat bare stage, or a multilevel unit set. The original production utilized a simple raked acting surface 20' by 20'. The back wall and stage floor were painted as a blue sky, which provided projection surfaces for a slide of Charles Boyer, various gobos (clouds, trees, windows) and a mirror ball. There was an old-fashioned wood-frame chalkboard on a wooden swivel yoke, and five vintage wooden school chairs (adult size); a large question mark was drawn on the chalkboard. A large window was suspended UL that could fly in or out when required. It helped to define the classroom, and presented a visual metaphor for the thematic statement made at the end of the Kindergarten Creed: "Remember...the biggest most important word of all—LOOK."

The setting should be an environment neutral enough for the details of the stories to emerge in the imagination of the listener. Although it may seem to be an obvious choice, the use of kindergarten or childlike images is not recommended. The opening sequence is the only part of the show that deals directly with kindergarten. After "Hide and Seek," the show deliberately leaves kindergarten behind. Most of the stories are adult in nature, and reflect adult observations of life. Pushing the kindergarten theme imposes a "cuteness" that could inappropriately skew the rest of the material, undercutting the potential for dramatic impact and trivializing the people and ideas that populate the world of the show

ABOUT THE LIGHTS

Creative lighting is very useful with this material, evoking a wonderful sense of mood and location, but the simplicity of the stories can get lost in excessive pyrotechnics. The actors' eyes and facial expressions are crucial assets to storytelling; therefore, strong visual focus should always be placed on the storytellers. Follow spots have proven useful in some productions. There are a few specific lighting effects mentioned in the stage directions. These are cues that have helped shape the drama of a story, or provide valuable rhythmic contributions to the flow of the show. In some instances, specific timing is discussed (i.e., the end of Beethoven). In most cases, clear punctuation created by the timing of a light cue at the end of each story is very useful. There are only a few places where full blackouts are suggested to provide a specific impact. Otherwise, going to a low-level transition light helps keep the show from getting too choppy.

ABOUT THE COSTUMES

There needs to be a strong level of identification between the actors and the audience, and the costumes are valuable in making this happen. They should suggest a sense of good taste and even an air of sophistication. In the original production, the actors wore casual colorful clothing, which was a *bit* funky. Coats, ties and dresses have also proven effective. Anything reminiscent of children's clothing, prints, styles, accessories is inappropriate. These are adults who think young, but must be taken seriously by the audience, and recognized as colleagues. An occasional costume piece (hat, glasses, purse) helps to establish the sense of a different character. See Appendix F for suggestions of costume pieces.

ADDITIONAL CHARACTER NOTES

FRED: Educated, paternal, witty, and a bit of a curmudgeon.

ED: Acerbic and wry; also able to exhibit a warm/romantic side. An excellent comedian with dramatic substance.

BRANISLAV: Idealistic, passionate. He is very funny, intelligent, with his own brand of sarcasm.

JILL: Warm, versatile and funny. Self-confident, with a true spark of life and a sense of irony. Possesses great depth.

KATHLEEN: Urbane and warm, with an air of wisdom from knowing how to live a full life. Has a real depth of character as well as a great sense of humor.

NARRATOR: Character is never seen, and possesses a friendly but authoritative nature. He or she is not intended to be a kindergarten teacher. The role was performed from the booth by the stage manager in the original production, but can also be performed by a separate actor or by the pianist/singer.

DAVID (optional onstage character): Friendly and charming, with a droll sense of humor. Conveys perspective that comes from intelligence and maturity. Because the score is extremely difficult to play, this individual must be an accomplished musician. In addition to acting as narrator, he/she may perform a curtain speech and/or audience warmup, in which case, he/she should be comfortable with audience banter. This character can also be offstage and never seen.

APPENDIX B
The Musical and Reduced-Musical Version for All Groups

THE MUSICAL VERSION

The sequence of stories and songs in the front of this script, and as listed in the table of contents, represents the "full-musical version" of the show. This order is designed to provide balance between sung and spoken material, with effective transitions from story to song. It is, however, possible to replace some songs with the spoken versions of the same stories if vocal skills warrant it. There is much more spoken in the show than sung, so acting skills should not be compromised in the casting. The two songs that truly benefit from strong singing abilities are "Reflect the Light" and "Tomb With a View." If necessary, some of the spoken material can be redistributed to allow for the casting of a performer who is primarily a singer.

THE REDUCED-MUSICAL VERSION
(a.k.a. the "non-musical" version)

The show can be effectively presented as a "reduced musical," or perhaps better labeled a "play with music." Although the show cannot be performed without some live music, the amount in this version is *significantly* reduced from the "full-musical" version. It is perfect for groups that do not normally present musicals. The "reduced musical" contains piano underscoring and transitions throughout, plus two songs: "The Kindergarten Song," and "Reflect the Light." It is just as successful with audiences as the "full-musical version."

The piano score clearly indicates what music is to be played in this version.

The two songs can be performed by one or more of the actors (all five, if desired). "The Kindergarten Song" is conversational

114

and not very demanding vocally. "Reflect the Light" is significantly more difficult: it has a wide range and calls for a singer comfortable with the "gospel" style. There are several ways the songs can be distributed within the cast (some discussed in the production notes); if you cast a strong singer in the role of Jill, it is possible for Kathleen to perform "The Bench," allowing Jill to be the featured singer on both songs. They can also be performed by the pianist if the piano can be positioned in such a way that he or she will have enough focus for this feature and not be obtrusive through the rest of the show. If you choose this option, it is beneficial to have the pianist perform the role of the narrator from a microphone at the piano. This is how it was performed in early productions, which proved to be successful.

If the narrator is a separate actor, it is also possible for him or her to sing either or both of these two songs, placing no singing demands whatsoever on the rest of the cast.

In most cases, it is useful to have the cast sing backup on "Reflect the Light."

If the singing demands of "Reflect the Light" cannot be met, it is possible to replace it with the short tag of "The Kindergarten Song" found in the appendix to the score. (It begins with "Think of the seed in the paper cup... " and continues to the end of the chorus.)

As a final alternative, it is possible to end the first act with "The Bench." This would provide the least amount of music, bringing the show as close as possible to a "non-musical."

SEQUENCE FOR THE REDUCED-MUSICAL VERSION

<u>ACT ONE</u>

1. Yes! Of Course I Can!
2. The Kindergarten Song *(Use one of the following options.*
   See appendix to piano score for Versions B and C)
   Version A: full version of song.
   Version B – Part 1: just verse 1 and chorus.
   Version C: pianist/narrator sings verse 1 as opening of show,
     before actors enter. Actors sing verses 2 and 3 *after* "Yes!
     of Course I Can!"
3. Cinderella
4. Hide and Seek
5. Larry Walters Flies
6. Charles Boyer *(Spoken version)*
7. Beethoven
8. Donnie the Leaf Raker
9. The Stuff in the Sink *(Spoken version)*
10. Problems and Inconveniences
11. The Bench
12. Reflect the Light *(Song)*
    Alternate endings for Act One, with less singing:
    a. "The Kindergarten Song" – the finale tag only
         (See appendix to score)
    b. The Bench

<u>ACT TWO</u>

13. Uh-Oh *(Spoken version)*
    Alternate openings for Act Two
    a. The Kindergarten Song *(Version B – Part 2: verses 2 and 3*
       and chorus)
    b. MOTB – Ensemble Version *(Found in Appendix E)*

14. MOTB *(Solo or Ensemble)*
15. Fathers and Sons
16. Pigeons
17. *(Both of these selections are effective but optional, and either one or both can be left out without hurting the show. Eliminating both helps keep the act under 60 minutes.)*
    a. Showdown in Grand Junction *(Found in Appendix E, follows "Pigeons")*
    b. What Do You Do? *(Spoken version found in Appendix E, done as intro to "Briefcase")*
18. The Briefcase
19. Howard
20. Christmas/Valentine's Day
21. Geek Dancing
22. Tomb With a View *(Spoken version)*
23. Are There Any Questions?
24. Reflect the Light—reprise *(Optional)*

NOTE ON VERSION C OF "THE KINDERGARTEN SONG"

If you are presenting the reduced-musical version of the show, and if you have chosen to have the pianist/narrator sing "The Kindergarten Song," you may want to consider Version C, suggested in the preceding running order. It plays as follows:

1. Open the show with the pianist/narrator singing the first verse and one chorus of "The Kindergarten Song." This functions as a welcome, and more importantly, introduces this particular character first. This is useful, since he or she stands apart from the rest of the cast. The chalkboard can be pre-set to show the Kindergarten Creed as the audience enters.

2. As pianist/narrator sings the word "LOOK," the actors enter as adult narrators, drinking in the classroom setting, with a sense of nostalgia. They sing "LOOK" twice (see appendix to piano score), as they gaze around the room.

3. SOUND CUE: a school bell. They rush to seats becoming kindergartners. Lights abruptly switch to scene light.

4. They perform "Yes! Of Course I Can!" according to stage directions.

5. When the school bell sounds at the end of the scene, they once again become the narrators who entered before the first school bell. The five actors now perform verses 2 and 3 of "The Kindergarten Song."

NOTE: The musical arrangement for Version C can be found in the appendix to the piano score.

APPENDIX C
Notes for Individual Stories

These are fairly random notes, some specific and some general. They are not meant to be comprehensive but more to cover specific questions and problems that have come up often in different productions. Some may seem obvious and others may provide new insight, but either way, they are only meant as information to fuel your own creativity and work with the material. It may be useful to read these notes again after you have gotten into the world of the stories more completely. They will most likely mean something different halfway through the rehearsal process.

YES! OF COURSE I CAN! (From *Uh-Oh*)
The three generations of characters in this scene are meant to be real, and not caricatures. There is an uninhibited sincerity and spontaneity to the children. The college students are cool and generate much comedy in their ability to wisecrack and cover up their insecurities. But some may also actually have sincere feelings about their inadequacies and wish things were different. The adults are so caught up in their insecurities that they only want to escape when asked to be creative or playful.

Each transformation is meant to evoke the laughter of recognition from the audience.

THE KINDERGARTEN SONG (From ... *Kindergarten*)
Because the Kindergarten Creed is so simple, it is important that the presentation include a sense of the more complex adult connotations behind these rules. The word "share" has many definitions, that range from personal interaction to global awareness, and it often refers to much more than material goods. Stress management can easily translate down to "take a nap

each day." The song has a strong sense of irony, as it intentionally pokes fun at the overly complex moral codes of adulthood and embraces the profound simplicity of the basics. These people are in truth sharing their life's philosophy, not performing a scene out of a kindergarten class. It is useful to read the entire original essay in the book that accompanies this creed, as well as the note from Robert Fulghum found in Appendix F.

The featured solos assigned to Jill can be switched with Kathleen, taking into consideration a balance in the distribution of material, and also which actress performs "Hide and Seek." And if it suits your production better, the first stanza can be redistributed among the entire cast.

The comic ending described in the stage directions was extremely successful in all productions that used it. It helps set the comic tone for much of what follows, especially Cinderella, and propels the show forward.

CINDERELLA (From *Uh-Oh*)

This version of the old Cinderella fairy tale is a comedy with heart. A new Cinderella is born in this story. One that each of the storytellers can celebrate, unlike the more traditional Cinderella for whom they have little respect. The traditional Cinderella is often portrayed as someone who sits around hoping she will be rescued from her oppression. Norman, however, is a Cinderella who asserts himself, takes control of his own destiny, and successfully moves into the spotlight of life. The teacher is the real Fairy Godmother, because she has the wisdom to empower this child. The ending is extremely heartfelt. It is a triumph for the cause of individuality in a world that often imposes conformity. "To thine own self be true." The storytellers are deeply touched by the validation bestowed on this child, who could have easily been kept on the outside. The joyous dance from his heart is a gift they will never forget.

The character of Norman is rather adult-like. He is intelligent, deeply earnest and sincere, and somewhat introverted. When Fred, the senior cast member, plays Norman, it brings dignity and humor to the character, but there may be another cast member who can bring something unique to Norman. Therefore, it is possible to switch Fred with any of the narrators. It is OK to cast a woman as Norman, but it is absolutely necessary that the gender of the character always remain male.

The character of the teacher is modern, grounded, and bright. Beware of the overly sweet and condescending cliché.

It is important to embrace the adult point of view and droll humor in the storytelling of Cinderella, avoiding anything overly cute and precious.

Norman and the teacher exist only in the world of the story and do not acknowledge the audience.

HIDE AND SEEK (From ... *Kindergarten*)

The storyteller uses humor and nostalgia to arrive at a more serious point. When she talks about the doctor who "hid too good," she must maintain her perspective and not be at all judgmental of his choice. She is not grieving herself, but instead, she is compassionate, as she points up the unfortunate irony of the situation.

Sardines is meant to be comical and fun, lifting the moment back up at this early point, in a show that has plenty of heavy moments.

This story could be performed by Jill (if Kathleen performs "The Bench") or by Fred.

LARRY WALTERS FLIES (From ... *Kindergarten*)

This is a delightful story of an outrageous act that says "everything is possible." Larry Walters was a real person, not a kook, but an ordinary guy. The narrators start off with a rather unassuming casualness, and then reveal the surprise of this outrageous event that both astonishes and delights them. Their final statements explain why Larry is their hero. This is ultimately a story about our ability to say "yes" to life.

Larry exists only in the world of the story and never connects with the audience.

Creating a visual comic button is useful to help propel the show forward.

CHARLES BOYER (From ... *Kindergarten*)

It is important to avoid extreme melodrama in the telling of Boyer's story. It is not meant to be a shocking or tragic lament but rather a complex love story which illustrates a more personal point. The storyteller is sharing the story because in a strange way, he was "touched" and "comforted" by it. In the final analysis, the piece is about how deeply the storyteller loves his own wife, with the last section being the most exposed and vulnerable.

Alternatively, Fred could perform this story. If he does, Ed should play the character of Larry Walters in the preceding story, since Larry is such a distinct persona. Ed can also then tell the story of "Donnie the Leaf Raker." If the sung version is presented, the actor should be conscious of keeping it very conversational, and not over-singing.

BEETHOVEN (From ... *Kindergarten*)

Beethoven is a story about joy. It is also about the dark side of the soul in contrast with the light of the spirit. The emotional architecture is particularly exciting to work with and benefits from bold and explosive choices.

The end of this piece is among the most transcendent moments in the show. It is the first time "light" is mentioned as a metaphor for truth, and in this case joy and beauty in the face of turmoil. The translation of the lyric in Beethoven's "Ode to Joy" is "Joy, radiant divine spark!" The gift of this great artist elevates the word "manalive" to a new level.

There is a playfulness to much of this piece. The storyteller expresses a contemporary, casual familiarity with "Old Mr. B" which is a means of disarming the audience. The humor allows the more dramatic moments like "...he just thought it" to stand out and resonate. This piece will suffer if the reverence of the ending is played out from the beginning.

"Beethoven" provides the first climax of Act One. When it is filled with humor, passion, and light, it can stop the show. The final "Ode to Joy" is intended to be an exhilarating moment in the theatre. A visual surprise (e.g., a sharp bright footlight casting a huge shadow on the back wall, à la *Fantasia*, or a crisp spotlight) helps deliver the punch.

DONNIE THE LEAF RAKER (From ... *Kindergarten*)

With dignity and integrity, Donnie challenges Fred's stubbornness and vanity. The comedy in this piece is found in Fred's struggle with his own ego, as he tries to hold onto his notion of winning the bargain. As he watches Donnie from his window, he tries to find justification for undoing Donnie's work, but every time he thinks the child may be slacking off, Donnie exhibits more integrity. The curmudgeon finally caves in, ultimately expressing his deep respect for Donnie's human dignity, perseverance, and grace. Fred gains a great lesson in letting go of his own attachments. He is in no way patronizing toward Donnie.

Within the architecture of this story, the storyteller is constantly digressing (describing the leaves, sparring with his wife, defending the importance of his scientific method). He can help the audience through this complex story by emphasizing which sections are part of the main plot, and which are colorful digressions.

The wife is confident in her point of view. She has tolerated her husband's somewhat eccentric arguments over the years and can recognize an elaborate evasion of work. This is a very solid, seasoned marriage, one that enjoys the sport of argumentation.

THE STUFF IN THE SINK (From *It Was on Fire ...*)

The teens in this story are fun to portray, but beware of overly exaggerated and clichéd characterizations. They are self-righteous and earnest in their point of view. Their stories in the song are very wordy, and benefit from clear storytelling. We have learned that overchoreographing this section is problematic. It is best when treated like a scene, not a "number."

For a more literal interpretation of the teenage point of view, it has proven effective to use Kathleen to illustrate "Mom's" role in their stories (e.g., cleaning the gunk BAREHANDED, fishing through the garbage, washing dishes). In this version of the story, Kathleen clearly plays three roles: Narrator, Mom, and Co-Graduation Speaker.

The teens can enter with skateboards, Walkmans, and other teen paraphernalia. The teen section can also be effectively presented without Mom or any props.

Take your time with the list presented by the graduation speakers. If they are evangelical in their seriousness, each item can get a good laugh.

PROBLEMS AND INCONVENIENCES (From *Uh-Oh*)

This story works best when it begins with Ed alone onstage, allowing the drama to emerge from his memory. Likewise, the impact of the story and its universality are strengthened by having Ed alone onstage at the end. The story is ultimately about how a mature man still carries the impact of Sig's wisdom, not about a young hotheaded college kid being put in his place.

Because the scene's climax happens during Sig's final monologue, he must be well lit, even though it takes place late at night. Sig and Branislav exist only in the world of the story and never speak to the audience.

At the line "And here I am again. A one-man war party at full cry," the original staging had the three men on a diagonal—BRANISLAV DL, ED C on a chair, FRED UR. FRED and

BRANISLAV talked "through" Ed as he remembered the incident, seeing it in his mind's eye. Each was in a separate pool of light.

THE BENCH (From *It Was on Fire...*)

This piece perhaps best demonstrates the structure of the stories in this show. The storyteller becomes a guide, gently leading the audience through the various ideas and images which allowed her to arrive at a moment in her own life when she grasped "a fragment of light—a glimpse of truth." She then reflects this "light" back to others, through her storytelling. This process is echoed in the song "Reflect the Light."

The storyteller has a unique friend in the person who left this bench. Some of her most insightful and intimate moments have been shared with this silent friend, whom she has never met.

The audience should feel as though they've gone for a walk with a close friend. Although the storyteller ponders her mortality with great depth, there is tremendous peace and serenity in her catharsis when she says "...It's okay."

The gentle comedy, suggested by the young lovers and the "milestone" birthday, helps to disarm the audience just before the climax. It also allows for a strong transition into "But it was on this bench."

This piece suffers if the reverence and drama are played from the beginning. She gently leads us to it in the end.

"The Bench" can also be performed by Kathleen, in which case, Jill could sing "Reflect the Light." Jill could then perform "Hide and Seek," if appropriate, allowing Kathleen to sing the lead solos in "The Kindergarten Song."

REFLECT THE LIGHT

This song was written to encapsulate the philosophy of the show. It foreshadows the ideas put forth in *Are There Any Questions?* and defines the action of every story. Because it is a melodic song, it is easy to get lost in the music and style. However, it is imperative that the singer clearly and passionately put forth the ideas expressed in the lyric.

It can be sung by Branislav, Jill, or whomever is most appropriate vocally. Although a little less desirable, it can also be sung by the full ensemble with no solo work at all. If Branislav sings the song, the staging should in no way suggest a romantic link between him and Jill.

UH-OH (From *Uh-Oh*)

The surprise of a chorus composed of short syllables like "Uh-oh" is a novelty and is meant to provide a lighthearted return from intermission. Although it may look complex on the page, with enough drilling even the most non-musical actor can catch on. If necessary, actors could hold their music in performance, under the guise of a formal choral presentation.

MOTB (From *It Was on Fire*)

MOTB is the comical zenith of the show. It kicks off Act Two with a burst of energy that fuels the remaining stories. It is important that it not take on a mean spirit, even though we all enjoy the human foibles depicted. There are no bad guys. Although it is not confessed until the end, the storyteller is very fond of this lady. In truth, it is everyone's story, since we are all capable of losing perspective, especially in the name of "joy." This woman carried excess to a new level, and it is helpful to lay this out for the audience with each item of excess. Ultimately, we discover the age-old lesson that no matter how much we try to control things, "life" will always interfere.

Even though this is the longest story in the show, rushing actually weakens it. Pauses are extremely valuable in allowing the audience to catch on to what is happening. More than any other piece, this one requires an audience before it can truly work.

MOTB can be performed either as a solo or as an ensemble piece (see Appendix E for ensemble version). Both versions have been effective. The solo version benefits from the delight of being in the hands of one skilled storyteller who possesses great comedic skills and charm. Ed, as the solo storyteller, is not meant to be the father of the bride. That relationship brings too much baggage to the situation. The perspective of a close friend of the family allows him to tell the story for all its worth.

The ensemble version allows the group to share the delight of the story but requires careful staging to keep the story clear. It is not meant to be a one-act play with characters, but instead, great storytelling with the occasional suggestion of specific characters.

FATHERS AND SONS (From *It Was on Fire ...*)

The three men in the cast play the same father at different stages of his life. The first two scenes are funny to everyone except the father. Both have poignant endings, but the comedy of these very human situations is what drives them. It is not hard for anyone who has been a parent or a child to relate to this tale, particularly if they are male.

The oldest father (Fred) has more perspective and appreciates the irony of his situation.

Each of the three actors should know the other two parts of the story in order to help establish themes that run through all three. Note how each father talks about "running" and someday "laughing" at all this.

Please allow us to share one of our favorite laughs in the show. It has seemed lame to everyone until hearing the response of the audience. When Fred says his son has a three-year-old son of his own, the audience laughs, knowing justice has been served. When he then laughs loudly with vindictive glee, he can get a second, even bigger laugh.

PIGEONS (From *Uh-Oh*)

The comical business in the stage directions helps to get this story off on the right foot. Once the two younger men have exited, Fred shares some of the irony of getting older. He then segues into the story.

Grandfather has an agenda at the top—he is going to be the most wonderful grandfather a child could ever hope for. In his attempt to execute this plan, the day becomes about him, and he inadvertently tries to "possess" his granddaughter. But when Sarah marches to her own drum, his agenda is quickly dashed, and his ego deflated. Once again, we are witness to the human comedy. He takes advantage of this ironic situation to examine what has just occurred. In the final analysis, he bestows Sarah with the dignity she deserves, as a person, not a cute child. He finds the real dynamic of their relationship: "To love something and to possess it ... are not the same thing."

YES

The song is intended to be wry and insightful, rather than plaintive.

If and when *ER* ever goes off the air, check the website (**allireallyneed.com**) for an update of that lyric (and any other passage in the script which becomes out-of-date).

THE BRIEFCASE (From *Uh-Oh*)

There is a playful spirit of innocence behind this story about human foibles. The storyteller knows she does not have to indict the neighbor—his own behavior indicts him. This story is about all of us and should not be told from a holier-than-thou perspective.

Ed and Kathleen exist only in the world of the story and do not acknowledge the audience. When blocking this scene, simple staging is recommended. The descriptive language does not require too much activity on the part of Ed and Kathleen. This story has also been successfully performed as a solo, without Ed and Kathleen.

HOWARD (From *Uh-Oh*)

The storyteller understands that the stakes are very high in this interrogation. He also knows he dare not lie by offering an insincere pat answer to the question "Do you believe in God?" so he couches his beliefs in this charming and funny story. The Meister Eckhart quote encapsulates much of his own philosophy.

The piece is very successful with a strong narrator (the person who supplied the voice in the opening scene) performing the interrogation, but it is also effective for Fred to play this role over a microphone from offstage.

The following staging is quite winning for Branislav's initial entrance, if the sightlines in the house allow for it: a light focuses on a two-inch hole in a trapdoor in the floor. A finger appears and moves around like a periscope. The finger quickly disappears. Branislav then slowly lifts the trapdoor with his head, as he peers out tentatively. He slowly emerges to about chest level while still standing in the trap. He then proceeds as marked in the script.

CHRISTMAS/VALENTINE'S DAY (From *Maybe, Maybe Not*)

This strong old lady has been called upon to experience tremendous growth at an age when she thought she had learned most of her lessons. She is quite resilient and has a sense of humor about the situation. However, when she tells her story, the emotional parts still sneak up on her. It was painful to lie to him, but his joy at hearing the stories was a precious gift. When she says "What harm," it recalls the sad and difficult moment of letting go as she surrendered to their new fate. She is delighted and deeply moved by her daughters' commitment to Christmas every time their father declares it. They give her great strength. The comedy within this piece is essential to its dramatic success.

The tragedy of his decline is balanced by the triumph of how they deal with it.

The character of the old man is not crazy in appearance. He comes across as a nice man who is truly in the Christmas spirit.

Ed begins the scene as a grump with a cold, and is transformed when he receives this "fragment of light," reflected back to him by this charming couple. This story functions as the dramatic turning point of Act Two.

Ed is the only one in this story who speaks directly to the audience.

GEEK DANCING (From *It Was on Fire...*)

This story unfolds very cleverly. The storytellers only drop subtle hints as to where the story is headed. It starts off with jokes which are somewhat irreverent and playfully poke fun at old age (from the point of view of both the young and the old). They get away with this, because they eventually honor old age with a very moving tribute to "geek dancing." When the mirror ball starts, the melody kicks in, and Fred begins to glide across the floor, *Kindergarten* offers one of its most magical moments. The two young people are witnesses to vintage love in motion. The Geek and the Geekess become the angels that were mentioned earlier in the story, and Jill and Branislav describe how their dance is truly "divine." The final ensemble dance, as described in the stage directions, is meant to be a burst of joy and romance and "Yes!"

A TOMB WITH A VIEW (From *From Beginning to End*)

The ideas in this story (and song) are complicated for the audience to digest. After the witty set-up, when the storyteller begins talking about the magnitude and complexity of space, he can help the audience by guiding them carefully through his discoveries of light, and the lasting power of the human spirit, and the eternal circle of energy from which they both emerge. His emotional depth is matched by his intellectual passion for these concepts.

ARE THERE ANY QUESTIONS? (From *It Was on Fire...*)

When the Narrator asks for any questions, Jill responds with "What is the meaning of life?" She is fully aware of the absurdity of the question, although she does not indicate that in her delivery. She knows the question will more than likely break the moment with laughter. This is a favorite trick of hers. She has used it at the end of long lectures or boring speeches to break things up and help everyone leave on a comical note. She will never forget the one time she got a serious answer.

The stage directions for this story are designed to help clarify what could seem confusing to the audience. The story is structured to be a very strong ensemble piece, but for the sake of clarity, Jill is given the strongest point of view. If it were to describe any one person's experience in Crete, it would be Jill's. Her relationship to Dr. Papaderos is very specific, but speaks for them all.

This is another story that could suffer if too much drama and reverence are played from the beginning. There are serious pieces of information (particularly about World War II) that require respect and weight, but since there is little comedy to give it energy, the ensemble needs to work together to keep it energized and moving.

Because the words of Dr. Papaderos are an extension of the individual thoughts of each of the actors, it is not effective to use anything resembling a Greek accent. This would interfere with the personal expression of the five people we have come to know over the course of the evening, as they each participate in the climactic story of the mirror. Dr. Papaderos' last line, spoken by Fred, reflects the philosophy of the entire show.

APPENDIX D
High School Version of the Script

All I Really Need to Know I Learned in Kindergarten is an excellent show for high schools, because it can be adapted to fit almost any situation. It can be performed with various numbers of actors and singers and can be adjusted in length to accommodate different kinds of events.

The show, as written, requires a minimum of five performers. It also will work effectively: 1.) as an ensemble show with up to ten actors, allowing students to appear multiple times (line distributions can be altered within stories to accommodate more narrators.); 2.) the show could also feature many more students if actors appear in only one or two stories each. In such cases, assignments are left up to the director. In the musical version, the actors can perform the songs, or a separate group of singers can be cast to perform them. This also allows for the possible collaboration between drama and choral departments.

The production notes found in Appendix A apply to all high school productions.

It is possible to add or delete stories according to the specific talents and circumstances of your drama and music programs.

We have included two pieces about aging and death ("Christmas Valentine's/Day" and "The Bench") in the High School version of the show, because young actors have been consistently enthusiastic about them; but the teacher or director can use his or her own judgment as to whether those pieces will truly resonate with the cast and audience. Either or both may be cut if they seem at all inappropriate to your production.

For a 30-minute cutting appropriate for competitions and one-act festivals, contact Dramatic Publishing.

Following are suggested sequences for musical and non-musical versions of the show.

FULL-LENGTH <u>MUSICAL</u> VERSION FOR HIGH SCHOOLS

<u>ACT ONE</u> (Approximately 55 minutes of material)

1. Yes! Of Course I Can! – Ensemble
2. The Kindergarten Song *(Song)* – Ensemble
3. Cinderella – Ensemble
4. Hide and Seek – Solo male or female, with ensemble walk–ons
5. Larry Walters Flies – Ensemble
6. The Solomon Islands – Ensemble with male or female solo feature *(found in Appendix E)*
7. Beethoven – Solo for male or female with small male or female feature.
8. The Stuff in the Sink *(Song)* – Ensemble with five solos
9. Donnie the Leaf Raker – Solo for male, with female feature. *(Story optional—can be cut from show)*
10. Problems and Inconveniences – Trio for three males
11. Reflect the Light *(Song)* – Major solo with ensemble backup, or multiple solos, or full ensemble.

<u>ACT TWO</u> (Approximately 60 minutes of material)

12. Uh–Oh *(Song)* – Ensemble
13. MOTB – Ensemble *(ensemble version found in Appendix E)*
14. Fathers and Sons – Trio for three males
15. What Do You Do? *(The Song)* – Ensemble *(found in Appendix E)*
16. Spider – Trio for two females and one male, or ensemble *(found in Appendix E)*
17. Howard – Onstage male or female solo with strong male or female feature offstage over sound system.
18. Christmas/Valentine's Day – Female solo with strong feature for two males, and walk–on for one female.

19. The Bench – Solo for male or female.
    (Story optional—can be cut from show)
20. Are There Any Questions? – Ensemble
21. Reflect the Light – Reprise *(Optional)*

NOTE: If the following pieces are cut, Act One should run approximately 45–50 minutes, and Act Two should run approximately 35-40 minutes: "Donnie the Leaf Raker," "The Bench," "Christmas/Valentine's Day."

FULL–LENGTH REDUCED-MUSICAL VERSION FOR HIGH SCHOOLS

ACT ONE (Approximately 55 minutes of material)

1. Yes! Of Course I Can! – Ensemble
2. The Kindergarten Song – Ensemble
    (full version, or just verse 1 and chorus)
3. Cinderella – Ensemble
4. Hide and Seek – Solo male or female, with ensemble walk-ons
5. Larry Walters Flies – Ensemble
6. The Solomon Islands– Ensemble with male or female solo
    feature *(found in Appendix E)*
7. Beethoven – Solo for male or female with small male or
    female feature at top
8. Donnie the Leaf Raker – Solo for male, with female feature
    (Story optional—can be cut from show)
 9. The Stuff in the Sink *(Spoken version)* – Ensemble
10. Problems and Inconveniences – Trio for three males
11. Reflect the Light *(Song)* – *(As ending for Act One)* Singing
    solo with ensemble backup, or multiple solos, or full ensemble

Alternate endings for Act One, which involve less or no singing:
    a. The Kindergarten Song – Chorus only
    b. Spider

ACT TWO (Approximately 60 minutes of material)

12. Uh-Oh *(Spoken version)* – Ensemble
Alternate ways to open Act Two:
>   a. The Kindergarten Song *(Verses 2 and 3 and chorus)*
>   b. MOTB *(Ensemble version. Note: If MOTB opens Act Two, Spider could be used to close Act One)*

13. Spider – Trio for two females and one male, or ensemble *(found in Appendix E)*
14. MOTB – Ensemble *(ensemble version found in Appendix E)*
15. Fathers and Sons – Trio for three males
16. Howard – Onstage male or female solo with strong male or female feature offstage over sound system
17. Christmas/Valentine's Day – Female solo with strong feature for two males, and walk-on for one female
18. The Bench – Solo for male or female
    (Story optional—can be cut from show)
19. Are There Any Questions? – Ensemble
20. Reflect the Light – Reprise *(Optional)*

NOTE: If the following pieces are cut, Act One should run approximately 50 minutes, and Act Two should run approximately 35-40 minutes: "Donnie the Leaf Raker," "The Bench," "Christmas/Valentine's Day."

The following pieces may be added, or substituted for any stories that may seem inappropriate to your specific circumstances:

1. Showdown in Grand Junction – Ensemble *(found in Appendix E.)*
2. The Briefcase – Solo for female or male with small feature for one male and one female. *(If performed, it is recommended to end it with the "BriefcasebnbgbbTag" found in Appendix E.)*

APPENDIX E
Alternate and Additional Stories and Songs

The following stories can be included for production if circumstances warrant the use of alternate or additional material.

1. Solomon Islands
2. Spider
3. Showdown in Grand Junction
4. MOTB – Ensemble Version
5. What Do You Do? – Spoken Version
6. What Do You Do? – Song
7. Briefcase Tag

SOLOMON ISLANDS
(Found in ... Kindergarten book)

([As written, this piece features Branislav, but it can be changed to feature any of the other performers.] PIANO MUSIC. Branislav stands C in his own world. The other four actors enter, sneaking up on BRANISLAV. When they have surrounded him, they take a collective breath and shout:)

ED, FRED, JILL, KATHLEEN. AAAAAAAAAAAAAAA-AAAHHHHHHHHHHHHHHHHHHHH!!!!!!!!!!!!!!!!!!

BRANISLAV. In the Solomon Islands in the South Pacific, some villagers practice a unique form of logging. If a tree is too large to be felled with an ax, the natives cut it down by yelling at it. I can't lay my hands on the article, but I swear I read it. Woodsmen with special powers creep up on a tree just at dawn and suddenly scream at the top of their lungs. *(The other three actors take a collective breath to shout, but BRANISLAV stops them before they get a chance.)* They continue this for thirty-five days. The tree dies and falls over. The theory is that the hollering kills the spirit of the tree. According to the villagers, it always works.

KATHLEEN. Ah, those poor naive natives.

FRED. Me? I yell at my wife.

JILL. I yell at the telephone.

ED. I yell at the lawn mower.

KATHLEEN. I yell at traffic.

BRANISLAV. At the dog.

KATHLEEN. At my kids.

JILL. And at machines.

ALL *(in mutual agreement).* Especially at machines! *(All ad lib kicking and shouting at a machine.)*

BRANISLAV. Machines and relatives get most of the yelling. Don't know what good it does; machines and "things" just sit there.

JILL. Even kicking doesn't always help.

BRANISLAV. As for people, well, the Solomon Islanders may have a point. Yelling at living things does tend to kill the spirit in them.

(PIANO TRANSITION—Use #8 in Piano score. Note: In the list of the various things they yell at, it is OK to substitute things that may be more appropriate to specific actors.)

stage right
(everyone21off)

SPIDER

(Found in ...Kindergarten book.)

(One of the actors draws a spider on the chalkboard. PIANO MUSIC: "The Eensy Weensy Spider." JILL is the neighbor, and KATHLEEN is the lady spider. They are seated on chairs DR, and DL. They mime FRED's narration. Piano creates sound effects under much of scene.)

FRED *(referring to JILL).* This is my neighbor. Nice lady. Coming out her front door on her way to work in her "looking-good" mode. She's locking her front door now and picking up her daily luggage: purse, lunch bag, gym bag for aerobics, and the garbage bucket to take out. She turns, sees me, gives me the big smiling:

JILL. "Hello!"

FRED. Takes three steps across the porch and goes:

JILL. "AAAAAAAGGGGGGGGGGGGHHHHHHHHHHHH!!!!!!!!!"

FRED. That's a direct quote. At about the level of a fire engine at full cry. Spider web. She has walked full force into a spider web. And the pressing question now of course is:

JILL. "Just where is the spider NOW?!"

FRED. She flings her baggage in all directions, and at the same time does a high-kick, jitterbug sort of dance, like a crazed stork in heat. Clutches at her face and hair. Tries opening the front door without unlocking it. Tries again. Breaks the key off in the lock. Runs around the house headed for the back door with a Doppler effect of:

JILL. "AAAAAGGGGHHHHHHaaaaaaaaaaaggggggggghhhhhhhh-AAAAAAGGGGHHHHHHH!!!!!!" *(After running around the house, she returns to her chair and sits.)*

BRANISLAV *(referring to KATHLEEN)*. Now a different view of this scene. *(PIANO MUSIC.)* This is the spider. Rather ordinary, medium gray, middle-aged lady spider. She's been up since before dawn, working on her web, and all is well.

KATHLEEN. "Nice day, no wind, dew point just about right to keep things sticky."

BRANISLAV. She's out checking the moorings and thinking about the little gnats she'd like to have for breakfast. Feeling good. Ready for action. All of a sudden all hell breaks loose—earthquake, tornado, volcano. The web is torn loose and wrapped around a frenzied moving haystack, and a huge piece of raw-but-painted meat is making a sound the spider never heard before:

JILL. "AAAAAAAAAAGGGGGGGGGGGGGGHHHHHHHHH!!!!!!!"

KATHLEEN. "It's too big to wrap up and eat later, and it's moving way too much to hold down."

BRANISLAV. Jump for it? Hang on and hope? Dig in?

KATHLEEN (*realizing what she caught*). "Human being."

BRANISLAV. She has caught a human being. And the pressing question now is:

KATHLEEN. "Where is it going, and what in God's name *on earth* will it do when it gets there?"

FRED. The neighbor lady thinks the spider is about the size of a lobster and has big rubber lips and poisonous fangs. The neighbor lady will probably strip to the skin and take a full shower and shampoo just to make sure it is gone—and then put on a whole new outfit just to make sure she is not inhabited.

BRANISLAV. The spider? Well, if she survives all this, she will really have something to talk about—

KATHLEEN. "The one that got away was THIS BIG!"

ED. There is a song about spiders. Everybody knows it...
(*PIANO ACCOMPANIMENT as he leads the other actors and the audience in "The Eensy Weensy Spider."*)

THE EENSY WEENSY SPIDER WENT UP THE WATER SPOUT
DOWN CAME THE RAIN AND WASHED THE SPIDER OUT
OUT CAME THE SUN AND DRIED UP ALL THE RAIN
AND THE EENSY WEENSY SPIDER WENT UP THE SPOUT AGAIN

What's the deal here? Why do we all know that song, and why do we keep passing it on from generation to generation? Especially when it puts spiders in such a favorable light. I mean out of all the times it has been sung, have you ever heard anybody go—

ALL. AAAAAAAAAAGGGGGGGGGGGGGGGGGGHHHHHHHHH-
IIIIHH!!!!!!!!!!!!!!!!!

ED. No. Maybe it's because it puts the life adventure in such clear and simple terms. Human beings have been coping with disasters and catastrophes for a long time. We are survivors. And we teach our kids about that. And maybe spiders tell their kids about it too, in their spider sort of way. *(BRANISLAV performs the Spider's actions, helped by the other actors. PIANO MUSIC.)* The small creature is alive and looks for adventure. Here's the drainpipe—a long tunnel going toward some light. The spider doesn't even think about it. Just goes. Disaster befalls it—rain, flood, powerful forces. And the spider is flushed down, and knocked far beyond where he started. Does the spider say: *forget it*

BRANISLAV. "Aw, to hell with it."

ED. No. Sun comes out—clears things up—dries off the spider. And the small creature goes over to the drainpipe, looks up and thinks:

BRANISLAV. "I really want to know what is up there."

ED. But it's a little wiser now—checks the sky first, looks for better toe-holds, says a spider prayer, and heads up through

ALL. Mystery

ED. toward the

ALL. Light

ED. and

ALL. Wherever.

(Spider climbs up behind the chalkboard. First we see his two hands, then another pair of hands, then a third pair of hands, then the spider's face, full of wonder and

amazement, as he arrives at the top. PIANO TRANSI-TION.)

(This story can be performed as a trio for JILL, KATH-LEEN, and BRANISLAV as follows: BRANISLAV does all the narration up to the song, with JILL and KATH-LEEN playing the characters. After the song, JILL and KATHLEEN split the narration and BRANISLAV becomes the spider. Note: In the original production, BRANISLAV played the neighbor, and ED played the lady spider, to great comic effect.)

SHOWDOWN IN GRAND JUNCTION
(Found in Maybe, Maybe Not)

(Works well in Act Two after "Pigeons." Can be performed as a quartet, or a duet between JILL and ED. Line distribution for duet is indicated in parentheses before each line. The chalkboard has a men's restroom symbol drawn on it. Behind the chalkboard JILL sits on a stool and manipulates a puppet that consists of a pair of pink tights, ankle socks and Maryjanes, with stuffing and 36-inch pieces of wood in each leg, which allow her to manipulate the feet. ED, in cowboy boots, interacts with the puppet. We see the two only from the knees down.)

BRANISLAV *(Jill).* GRAND JUNCTION, COLORADO. Hot afternoon in mid-July. Local newspaper headline says: POWER SHORTAGE IN GRAND JUNCTION.

FRED *(Ed)*. In the men's room in the local airport passenger terminal, another kind of power problem is in progress. From behind the stall door comes:

JILL. "No, no, no, no, no. I won't. I won't."

BRANISLAV *(Jill)*. Followed by:

ED. "Please. Do it for Daddy?"

JILL. "No, no, no, no!"

FRED *(Ed)*. The seven men using the facilities turn their faces in unison toward the stall door.

BRANISLAV *(Jill)*. In the opening at the bottom of the door, two sets of feet can be seen.

FRED *(Ed)*. A large pair, in polished brown cowboy boots. *(Man's feet in boots appear.)*

BRANISLAV *(Jill)*. And a much smaller pair in black patent leather shoes. *(Little girl's feet appear ... with attitude.)*

FRED *(Jill)*. The encounter continues:

ED. "Look, I know you have to go. You go every day. If you don't go now, you'll have to go when we're standing in line, or after we're strapped into our seats, or when we're thirty-five-thousand feet in the air, and it's a small plane with no potty, and you'll probably mess your pants, and we'll have to clean you up when we're way up there, and you don't want to have to do that, and I don't want to have to do that, so why don't you just go now like a good girl?"

JILL. "No ... This is the boy's place."

ED. "I know, but Daddy can't go in the girl's room."

JILL. "No."

ED. "What will Mommy and Grandma say when we get off the plane and you've messed your pants and you're crying and I'm mad? They won't be glad to see us."

JILL. "Yes, they will."

ED. "We're going to miss our plane if you don't go now."

JILL. "I don't care."

ED. "Am I going to have to spank you?"

JILL. "No."

ED. "Then please, please at least try."

JILL. "No."

ED. "If you go, I'll buy you an ice cream."

JILL *(stamps her foot)*. "No."

ED. "I'll buy you a present—you can pick it."

JILL *(stamps her foot)*. "No."

ED. "I'll give you a dollar."

JILL *(raises her foot, hesitates as she considers, then stamps her foot)*. "No."

ED *(gets down on his knees)*. "Please try—just as a favor to Daddy."

JILL. "No."

ED. "Well bygod you've just got to do it, that's all there is to it. You're going to sit on this pot until something happens." *(He picks up the puppet.)*

JILL. "Noooooooooooooooooooo."

ED. "You little..." *(She kicks him.)* "Aw, hell." *(Puppet feet disappear.)*

FRED *(Jill)*. The stall door swings open. A five-year-old girl emerges in tears, her lips puckered in fierce refusal and her mind set in cement as she marches solemnly past the onlookers and out the door. *(This is indicated by light, or suggested by FRED.)*

BRANISLAV *(Ed)*. Her father follows. *(ED appears from behind chalkboard.)* Big man in a black Stetson. Red-faced mad. Embarrassed. Defeated. Humiliated. Nobody pushes him around. Nobody tells him "NO."

ED. But his five-year-old girl-child has done it. And she has not done her "business." And there's going to be trouble in the air and a fracas when they get to Denver. *(ED exits, chasing after his daughter.)*

FRED *(Jill)*. The impromptu Committee of Wise Men who have witnessed this drama, and who remain behind in the sudden quiet of the men's john, render their judgments. *(During the following sequence, they mime activity at urinals, sinks, and paper towel dispensers.)*

BRANISLAV *(Ed)*. "Sure glad I ain't in his shoes."

FRED *(Jill)*. "That kid's gonna 'splode at thirty-five thousand feet."

BRANISLAV *(Ed)*. "Women—don't know what's worse trouble, the little ones or the big ones."

FRED *(Jill)*. "If it had been me, I'd have given her a banana split, a hundred dollars, all the presents she could carry, and a U.S. Savings Bond before I would have gotten on that plane with her."

(ED reentering [as if] being pulled by his daughter.)

ED. Later, the man and his child headed back to the men's room in a big hurry. This time she *had* to go. *(He steps behind chalkboard. The feet of the puppet are seen dangling as she sits. ED then steps back onstage from behind chalkboard.)* They missed the plane. *(PIANO MUSIC.)*

BRANISLAV *(Jill)*. Father and daughter will survive this ordeal. Time will turn it into family legend. This is the kind of story a father will save to tell about his daughter at the rehearsal dinner of her wedding. It will be funny, especially with the embellishments fathers are prone to make. This time it is she who will be embarrassed.

FRED *(Ed)*. But the father will make it clear, as fathers sometimes do, that he's proud of this independent-minded child—always has been—and the groom had better understand that he's marrying a strong woman, who has been thinking for herself for a long time. *(SOUND CUE: Toilet flush. BLACKOUT. PIANO TRANSITION.)*

(Note: The following are three alternate staging solutions which have proven successful for this story. 1.) ED in cowboy boots, and JILL in Maryjanes stand U of chalkboard, and enact the scene. The audience sees them from the knees down. They emerge and exit after the showdown and return for the end. 2.) A square of light is projected onto the floor, ED acts out the scene with an invisible little girl, while JILL provides the voice from the shadows. 3.) JILL and ED divide up all the narration, as well as perform the dialogue, while BRANISLAV in cowboy boots and KATHLEEN as puppeteer nonverbally provide the feet from the knees down on a separate puppet stage, or behind the chalkboard. JILL and ED enact the characters when they emerge from the stall, then transform into the men left behind in the restroom. The puppet stage is used again when father and daughter return to the restroom. This provides a duet for JILL and ED. The line distribution for version #3 is indicated in parentheses.)

(Used as <u>optional</u> intro to "The Briefcase" in "reduced-musical" version of the show. Replaces the song "Yes!")

(PIANO MUSIC: JILL, KATHLEEN, ED and BRANIS-LAV enter, and take their seats as in the opening scene.)

NARRATOR. What do you do?

JILL *(musing over the question)*. What do you do? *(To audience.)* Your basic strangers-on-a-plane question.

BRANISLAV *(to audience)*. Comes up at the PTA potluck ...

KATHLEEN *(to audience)*. ... and corporate cocktail parties ...

ED *(to audience)*. And just about any other stand-around-and-make-small-talk situation you get into.

JILL *(to audience)*. Say what you are paid to do, and we'll know who you are, and how to deal with you.

NARRATOR. What do you do?

KATHLEEN *(to narrator)*. I'm a singer. *(To audience and narrator.)* Not only do I not get paid to sing, but in some cases friends might offer to pay me not to sing. Nevertheless, I love to do it. In the shower, driving to work, while I'm working—whenever. I sing. It's what I do. I loved it when my children were young, and had no musical standards. We'd sing all the time. It didn't matter that we didn't always know all the words, or have the tune just right—we made it up. We singers are not thrown by technicalities. Singers are those who sing. Period.

NARRATOR. What do you do?

WHAT DO YOU DO? *(Spoken Version)*
(Found in It Was on Fire ...)
(Used as <u>optional</u> *intro to "The Briefcase" in "reduced-musical" version of the show. Replaces the song "Yes!")*

ED *(to narrator)*. I'm a prince.

NARRATOR. A prince?

ED *(to narrator and audience)*. Yeah. Just this morning my wife said, *(Mimicking his wife's insulting tone.)* "Sometimes you're a real prince." And you know what? I've been feeling "Princely" ever since.

NARRATOR. What do you do?

BRANISLAV *(to audience and narrator)*. Marcel Duchamp, the sculptor and painter, who was a fixture in the world of fine art during the period before 1940, was quite frustrated by the implications of the "what do you do" inquiry. He would answer, "I am a *respirateur*"—a breather. He explained that he did more breathing than anything else, and was very very good at it too. After that, people were usually afraid to ask what else he did. *(The remainder of the scene is spoken to the audience.)*

JILL. What I do is more than a job title, it is *literally* how I spend my time. *(Rising.)* In my life, I figure I've spent twenty-five hundred hours brushing my teeth,

BRANISLAV *(rising)*. thirty thousand hours in traffic,

ED *(rising)*. thirty-five thousand hours eating,

KATHLEEN *(rising)*. two hundred seventeen thousand hours at work,

JILL *(stepping D)*. eight hundred seventy thousand hours just coping with odds and ends:

ED *(stepping D)*. filling out forms

BRANISLAV *(stepping D)*. paying bills

KATHLEEN *(stepping D).* getting dressed and undressed

JILL. being sick.

BRANISLAV. When you finish with all the arithmetic, there's not a lot of time left over. *(He looks at his watch and exits.)*

ED. Somehow, in the middle of it all, you have to find the time to fit in the "good stuff"... *(He exits.)*

KATHLEEN. Making a living and having a life, are *not* the same thing. *(She exits.)*

(Direct segue to "The Briefcase.")

"WHAT DO YOU DO" *(The Song)*
(Found in It Was on Fire...)

(There is a frenetic, repetitive musical introduction à la Phillip Glass, during which the four actors enter. In a semi-robotic style, they punch a time-clock, and begin a simple mime of a work task that can be repeated several times until the end of the music. Examples: word processing, jackhammer, driver, traffic cop, etc. At the end of the intro, they all freeze in a work tableau.)

NARRATOR. What do you do?

JILL (musing over the question, she repeats it). What do you do?

YOUR BASIC COCKTAIL CONVERSATION —
FILL IN THE BLANK MARKED "OCCUPATION"—

ED.

A COURTEOUS WAY OF DEMANDING
DETAILS OF YOUR SOCIAL STANDING.

KATHLEEN *(taking out an actual business card, she passes it to BRANISLAV).*
DESCRIBE YOUR DAILY GRIND,

BRANISLAV *(passing the card to ED).*
SAY WHAT YOU'RE PAID TO DO,

ED *(passing the card to JILL).*
AND WE'LL KNOW WHO YOU ARE

JILL.
AND HOW TO DEAL WITH YOU.
When I ask people what they do, I usually get a little piece of stiff paper like this. *(She holds up the card.)* It summarizes their identity. Name, company, title, address, lots of numbers: phone, telex, E-mail, beeper and fax. A business card. I debated for a long time about getting one myself.

BRANISLAV *(to KATHLEEN).* So ... What do you do? *(KATHLEEN acts the part of the business executive. She takes out another card, and hands it to him. BRANISLAV first sings to audience.)*
A LADY GAVE ME HER BUSINESS CARD NOT TOO LONG AGO;
(Reading card.)
IT SAID SHE'S VICE PRESIDENT FOR SYSTEMS ANALYSIS OF UNICO.
(To KATHLEEN.)
I SAID, "OKAY, BUT WHAT IS IT YOU ACTUALLY DO?"
(To audience.)
SHE POINTED AT THE CARD, AS IF I'D SOMEHOW MISSED THE CLUE.

(To KATHLEEN.)
> **"BUT WHAT WOULD I SEE YOU DO ALL DAY IF**
> **I FOLLOWED YOU AROUND?"**

(To audience.)
> **FOR A LONG TIME, WE STOOD THERE AND I**
> **LISTENED TO HER EXPOUND.**

I still don't really know what she does. *(KATHLEEN grabs card from BRANISLAV and walks away.)* I'm not sure she does, either.

NARRATOR. So what exactly do you do?

ED.
> **I CAN'T DESCRIBE IN A WORD OR TWO**
> **THE SUM TOTAL OF WHAT I DO.**
>
> **THE OTHER DAY, WHEN I WAS DOING SOME**
> **BUSINESS AT MY BANK,**
> **FILLING OUT A FORM, I WROTE DOWN**
> **"PRINCE" IN THE OCCUPATION BLANK.**
> **WELL, WHY NOT? JUST THAT MORNING, MY**
> **WIFE HAD SAID,**
> **"SOMETIMES YOU'RE A REAL PRINCE"**
> **AND YOU KNOW WHAT? I'VE BEEN FEELING**
> **PRINCELY EVER SINCE.**

(MUSIC continues under dialogue.)

The clerk couldn't handle it. And we had a friendly argument that goes to the heart of this matter of identity: Is my occupation what I get paid money for, or is it something larger and richer— more a matter of what I *am* or how I *think* about myself.

KATHLEEN. A job title doesn't even come close to answering the question "What do you do?" Marcel Duchamp, the sculptor and painter who was a fixture in the world of fine art during the period before 1940, was equally frustrated by the implications of the standard "What do you do" inquiry. He would answer, "I am a *respirateur*"—a breather. He explained that he did more breathing than anything else, and was very, very good at it, too. After that, people were usually afraid to ask him what else he did.

NARRATOR. What do you do?

JILL. I know, I know. We can't go around handing out two-hundred page descriptions of our lives every time someone asks what we do. But a job is not the same as a life.

WHAT IF WE USE THE WORD "OCCUPATION" TO MEAN WHATEVER MAKES US FEEL HAPPY OR USEFUL TO THE HUMAN ENDEAVOR? MAKING A LIVING AND HAVING A LIFE ARE NOT THE SAME THING. LIVING *THE* GOOD LIFE AND LIVING *A* GOOD LIFE ARE NOT THE SAME THING.

NARRATOR. So... What do you do?

JILL. What I do is literally how I spend my time.

IN MY LIFE, I FIGURE I'VE SPENT TWENTY-FIVE HUNDRED HOURS BRUSHING MY TEETH

BRANISLAV.

THIRTY THOUSAND HOURS IN TRAFFIC,

ED.
> **THIRTY-FIVE THOUSAND HOURS EATING,**

KATHLEEN.
> **TWO HUNDRED SEVENTEEN THOUSAND
> HOURS AT WORK,**

JILL.
> **EIGHT HUNDRED SEVENTY THOUSAND HOURS
> JUST COPING WITH ODDS AND ENDS:**

ED.
> **FILLING OUT FORMS,**

BRANISLAV.
> **PAYING BILLS,**

JILL.
> **GETTING DRESSED AND UNDRESSED,**

ED.
> **BEING SICK.**

JILL.
> **WHEN YOU ADD IT UP, THERE'S NOT A LOT OF
> TIME TO SPARE.
> YOU HAVE TO FIT THE GOOD STUFF IN
> SOMEWHERE.**
> So now I have a business card. Finally figured out what
> to put on it. One word. *(She takes out a business card
> revealing her name.. Speaks.)* "Jill"
> **THAT'S MY OCCUPATION—NO APOLOGY**

(The actors take out business cards revealing their names. Each says their first name: "Ed," "Branislav," "Kathleen.")

**TO BE THE MOST
[JILL—BRANISLAV—ED—"KATHLEEN"] I
CAN BE.**
(Can continue on, or skip to: "I AM A LIVING MIR-ACLE.")
Which means being a
Daughter,
Mother,
Sister,
Aunt,

JILL & ED. Who is also a Neighbor,
ED. Confidante,
ED & BRANISLAV. Dreamer,
BRANISLAV. Wisher,
  Laugher,
  Singer,
BRANISLAV & KATHLEEN. Painter,
KATHLEEN. Doctor,
  Burger-Slinger,
ALL. And on, and on, and on.
  **I AM A LIVING MIRACLE—SO ARE YOU—
  A FULL-BLOWN THREE-RING CIRCUS—
  THAT'S WHAT WE DO!**

MOTB

(Alternate Ensemble Version: Can function as opening to Act Two in "reduced-musical" version of show.)

(PIANO MUSIC: "Here Comes The Bride" as intro. The actors are seated on their chairs U in one or two rows following "Uh-Oh." They react to the music as if they were in church. They go back and forth between the roles of narrators and wedding guests. The narrators should be very aware of the story as a whole, and sensitive to pauses as well as the overall comic rhythm.)

ED. Most weddings are such comedies. *(Pause.)*

BRANISLAV. Not that they are intended as such. But since weddings are high state occasions involving amateurs under pressure ... everything NEVER goes right.

FRED *(takes his chair and places it DLC to represent the MOTB. As they talk about the MOTB, they refer to the chair).* The central figure in this drama was the mother of the bride, the MOTB. Not the bride and groom or minister. Mother. Usually a polite, reasonable, intelligent, and sane human being, Mother was mentally unhinged by the announcement of her daughter's betrothal. I don't mean she was unhappy as is often the case. To the contrary. She was overcome with joy. And just about succeeded in overcoming everybody else with her joy. *(Steps aside.)*

ED *(crossing down to stand behind MOTB chair).* Nobody knew it, but this lady had been waiting with a script for a production that would have met with Cecil B. DeMille's approval. A royal wedding fit for a princess bride. The father of the bride began to pray...for an elopement.

(During the next sequence, chairs are set up to represent the pews in the church, with a center aisle. A bridal runner has been preset DC.)

KATHLEEN *(beginning the long list of excesses, which they all help to emphasize)*. She had seven months to work, and no detail was left to chance or human error. Everything that could be engraved was engraved. *(Places a chair and sits.)* There were teas...

JILL *(places a chair and sits)*. and showers...

BRANISLAV *(places a chair and sits)*. ...and dinners.

FRED. An eighteen-piece brass-and-wind ensemble was engaged.

ED *(places a chair)*. The bride and groom met with the minister only three times. The MOTB was in his office more than the cleaning lady.

JILL *(after a pause, rises)*. Not only were the bridesmaids' outfits made to order, but the tuxedos for the groom and his men were bought—not rented, mind you. Bought.

FRED *(rises)*. And, if all that wasn't enough, the engagement ring was returned to the jeweler for a larger stone, quietly subsidized by the MOTB. When I say the lady came unhinged, I mean UNHINGED. *(PIANO MUSIC: Roll.)*

BRANISLAV *(rises)*. The juggernaut of fate rolled down the road, and the final hour came.

(PIANO MUSIC: Fanfare. They rush to their places as guests seated in the church. Someone steps D and pulls

*the bridal runner from DC to UC, establishing the
church. Another person gets extra chair(s) from offstage
and places them to complete the symmetry of the pews.
There should be empty chairs D to the right and left of
the bridal runner; one for the MOTB, the other for the
mother of the groom. MUSIC stops as last person gets to
their seat.)*

JILL. Guests in formal attire packed the church. *(She and
BRANISLAV sit.)*

KATHLEEN. Enough candles were lit to bring daylight
back to the evening. *(She sits.)*

ED. In the choir loft, the orchestra gushed great music. *(PI-
ANO MUSIC. He sits.)*

FRED [or ED] *(referring to the aisle as he crosses UC and
stops).* And the mighty MOTB coasted down the aisle
with the grandeur of an opera diva at a premiere performance. *(After finishing the preceding line, he steps
onto the bridal runner, then takes his time strutting
down the aisle as the MOTB, full of regality and false
modesty. He speaks as he sits in the MOTB's chair.)*
Never did the mother of the bride take her seat with
more satisfaction. She had done it. *(He acts out the following.)*

BRANISLAV. She glowed,

JILL. beamed,

ED. smiled

KATHLEEN. and sighed. *(FRED sighs. She rises.)* The
music softened, and nine—count them, nine—chiffon-
draped bridesmaids lockstepped down the long aisle ...
(She sits.)

FRED *(drops the character of the MOTB for the remainder of the story, leaving her image to the imagination of the audience. He rises and crosses back to another empty seat as he gestures toward the altar).* ...while the groom and his men marched into place.

ED. Finally, the wedding march thundered from the orchestra! *(PIANO MUSIC.)* <u>Here comes the bride</u>. *(All rise and turn toward the back of the church in anticipation. ED indicates for them to sit back down because there is still more parade before the bride actually appears.)* Preceded by four enthusiastic mini-princesses chunking flower petals, *(All rise again, but ED gestures for them to sit back down because there is still more parade.)* ...and two munchkin ring bearers—one for each ring.

JILL. The congregation rose and turned in anticipation. *(All rise as narration suggests.)* "Ah, the bride."

She had been dressed for hours... if not days. *(Pause.)*

No adrenalin was left in her body. *(Pause.)*

ED *(lights shift to ED as he crosses DR. The others drift R, dropping their roles as guests, and becoming narrators, as they observe ED acting out the bride's activity. The others look on and report their observations as ED continues the mime).* Left alone with her father in the reception hall of the church while the march of the maidens went on and on, the bride had walked along the tables loaded with gourmet goodies, and absent-mindedly sampled first the little pink and yellow and green mints. Then she picked through the silver bowls of mixed nuts and ate the pecans.

KATHLEEN *(pause).* Followed by a cheeseball or two,

BRANISLAV *(pause).* ...some black olives,

JILL *(pause).* ...a handful of glazed almonds,

FRED *(pause).* ...a little sausage with a frilly toothpick stuck in it,

KATHLEEN *(pause).* ...a couple of shrimps blanketed in bacon,

BRANISLAV *(pause).* ...and a cracker piled with liver paté.

ED *(dropping the character of the bride, he steps into the role of the father).* To wash this down—a glass of pink champagne. Her father gave it to her. To calm her nerves. *(All return to their seats, becoming guests again. The MOTB's chair remains empty; BRANISLAV steps onto the runner UC.)*

BRANISLAV. What you noticed, as the bride stood in the doorway, was not her dress, but her face. *(Pause.)* White. *(Pause. He begins to walk down the aisle.)* For what was coming down the aisle was a living grenade with the pin pulled out. *(Pause.)* The bride... *(He stops D next to the MOTB chair. MUSIC stops.)* ...threw up. *(Pause. Gestures to MOTB chair.)* Just as she walked by her mother. *(He steps U.)*

ED *(after a pause, he rises, steps D).* And by "threw up," we don't mean a polite little ladylike urp into her handkerchief. She puked. *(Pause.)* There's just no nice word for it. I mean, she *hosed* the front of the chancel— *(Pause.)* —hitting two bridesmaids, the groom, a ring bearer, and the minister. *(Pause.)* I am quite sure of the details. We have it all on videotape. *(Pause.)* Three cameras' worth. *(Pause.)* The MOTB had thought of everything.

JILL. Having disgorged her hors d'oeuvres, champagne, and the last of her dignity, the bride went limp in her father's arms, while her groom sat down on the floor where he had been standing, too stunned to function.

FRED *(rises and steps to just above MOTB chair, referring to her).* And the mother of the bride moaned, slumped over and passed out cold. *(Pause.)*

BRANISLAV. There was a fire drill then and there at the front of the church that only the Marx Brothers could have topped. *(PIANO MUSIC starts and pandemonium begins as they all rush about, shouting.)*

ED. Groomsmen rushed about heroically,

KATHLEEN. mini-princess flower girls squalled,

JILL. bridesmaids sobbed,

BRANISLAV *(from DC).* and people with weak stomachs headed for the exits. *(All rush U and freeze. Slow MUSIC begins as he speaks.)* The smell... of fresh retch... drifted across the church.

FRED *(after a pause, and without giving away the joke, he steps toward the mother of the groom's chair DRC).* Only two people were seen smiling. One was *(Gestures to her chair.)* ... the mother of the groom.

ED *(after a pause).* And the other was... the father of the bride!

KATHLEEN *(after a pause, crosses D).* What happened next? Well, we all went back to real life. Guests were invited to adjourn to the reception hall, *(ED and FRED join the others U.)* though they did not eat or drink as much as they might have in different circumstances. *(Pause.)* The bride was consoled, cleaned up, fitted out with a bridesmaid's dress, and hugged and kissed a lot by the groom. She'll always love him for that. When he said "For better or worse," he meant it. *(Pause. All return to their seats. PIANO MUSIC.)* The cast was reassembled where we left off, a single flute played a quiet air, the words were spoken and the deed was done. Everybody cried, as people are supposed to do at weddings, mostly because the groom held the bride in his arms through the whole ceremony. And no groom ever kissed a bride more "tenderly" than he. *(She sits.)*

FRED. If one can hope for a wedding that it be memorable, then theirs was a raging success. *(Pause.)* NOBODY who was there will EVER forget it.

JILL. They lived as happily ever after as anyone does— happier than most, in fact. *(Assisted by someone, she clears the bridal runner and it is tossed offstage.)* They have been married about twelve years now, and have three lively children.

BRANISLAV. But that's not the end of the story. On the tenth anniversary of this disastrous affair, a party was held. *(KATHLEEN says "Ding-Dong," as everyone grabs chairs and arranges them into party formation in front of imaginary TV sets, and sits, leaving the MOTB's chair in its original position.)* A feast was laid, best friends invited...

ED *(still standing).* ...and three TV sets were mustered. *(Pause.)* Remember there were three video cameras at the scene of the accident. All three tapes were shown at once. The effect was...pretty interesting. Especially with the running commentary and the stop-action stuff that is a little gross when seen one frame at a time.

(If "Uh-Oh" is performed, the following excerpt should be spoken as a response to what they are all watching on the video. If it is not performed, skip to ED's line after "Yuck!")

FRED. Ugh!

KATHLEEN. Uh-oh.

BRANISLAV. Ick!

KATHLEEN & FRED. Uh-oh.

JILL. Pew!

KATHLEEN, BRANISLAV, FRED. Uh-oh.

ED. Sheesh!

JILL, KATHLEEN, BRANISLAV, FRED. Uh-oh.

KATHLEEN. Yikes!

JILL, BRANISLAV, ED, FRED. Uh-oh.

FRED. Ewww!

JILL, KATHLEEN, BRANISLAV, ED. Uh-oh.

BRANISLAV. Whoa!

JILL, KATHLEEN, ED, FRED. Uh-oh.

JILL. Awww!

KATHLEEN, BRANISLAV, ED, FRED. Uh-oh.

ALL. YUCK!

ED. The part that got cheers and toasts was when the camera focused on the grin of the father of the bride as he contemplates his wife being revived.

FRED. I really like this part of the story, not because of the party. But because of who organized it. Of course. The infamous MOTB.

BRANISLAV. The mother of the bride is still at it, but she's a lot looser these days.

KATHLEEN. She not only forgave her husband and everybody else for their part in the debacle, she forgave herself.

ED. And nobody laughed harder at the videotapes than she.

FRED. There's a word for what she has. Grace.

ED. And that's why that same grinning man has been married to her for forty years.

JILL. And why her daughter loves her still.

(PIANO MUSIC: Wedding Recessional. They exit removing some of the chairs, with one or two of the actors tossing a handful of rice or confetti into the audience.)

BRIEFCASE TAG

(Alternate addition to end of "The Briefcase." Recommended only for high school productions or other special circumstances.)

(KATHLEEN and ED exit in opposite directions.)

JILL. The owner of the "veldtmobile" is a little distant these days. I hear it cost him $400 to have his hood repainted. I see that he has a new briefcase, just like the last one.

He's not a bad guy. In a way, I see my face in his mirror. I get pretty fuzzed out sometimes too. But it's less embarrassing to talk about how he runs *his* life, than to talk about the cartoon quality of my *own.*

In the meantime, he's unhappy with us. I hear he thinks we ruined his day. And thinks we cost him time and money, and kept him from getting his business done.

I can't speak for him, but when it comes to my own business, there's a very old "profit and loss" statement that I like to keep taped to my wall: "What does it profit a man if he gain the whole world and lose his soul?"

PRESHOW

A pre-show "warm-up" has served effectively to establish rapport with the audience, breaking down any sense of formality. We developed the following script during the original production. You are welcome to use it, or create your own "warm-up," or eliminate it altogether—whatever is appropriate for your theatre. Most productions of the show have been performed successfully with no warm-up at all.

This script may sound awkward on paper, but it was presented in three different productions with great success. It seems to require a somewhat deadpan yet playful presentation. It relies heavily on the personality of the performer and may not suit all individuals playing the role of Pianist/Narrator. It is essential that it come off not as a childish ploy, but as droll fun.

The Pianist/Narrator enters with a Polaroid camera and begins to photograph the audience, in the disarming and humorous style of a silent clown (like Bill Irwin). Before he takes the first photo, he assesses the light, discerns that it is too dark, crosses to the proscenium and pulls a large, imaginary light switch which is out of sight of the audience but makes an audible sound. The theatre is flooded with light. He looks over the crowd, and begins photographing them. He holds the camera to his face and waves, trying to get the audience to wave back at the camera. He takes a comb from his pocket, and runs out to an audience member on an aisle as if to comb his/her hair, but then chooses to pick a piece of lint off the audience member's garment instead. As he holds the camera up to photograph another section of the house, he hesitates, then gestures for them to all move in closer for the shot, disregarding the impossibility of what he's requesting. *(Feel free to develop other silent jokes to warm up the audience, and let them know they are in for something different.)* As the Pianist/Narrator takes each photo, he places it on the stage floor or on one of the chairs to develop. When he is done taking photos, he speaks for the first time.

"Hi, I'm_____, and I'll be sitting over there at the piano in just a moment. I'd like to welcome you to *(Name of theatre.)* and tonight's performance of *All I Really Need to Know I Learned In Kindergarten.* I hope you don't mind my taking your picture. Anyone here running from the law? Anyone having a bad hair day? Anyone here with your "cousin," if you know what I mean? While we're waiting for these pictures to develop, I'd like to pass on some valuable information... *(Any standard curtain speech can be inserted here.)* Now let's take a look at these photos. Wow, these turned out great. You are a very glamorous group. Much better looking than last night's audience. You turned out particularly well. *(Indicating someone in the front row.)* Here, take a look. *(He shows person in the front row. Then he holds the photos up and asks:)* Can you all see these in the back? I suppose you're wondering why I took your pictures. Well, you may have noticed as you sat here waiting for the show to begin that there are photos and bios of actors and staff members in your playbill, and 8x10 glossies of the performers in the lobby. Well, we decided that for this production we'd do something a little different, and acknowledge a group of people who are also a major part of this evening's performance... *(He holds up the photos, indicating the audience as this compo-*

nent.) So, during the first act we'll be passing these around backstage ... for our own amusement; then we'll put them up on the marquee in the lobby with the other participants in tonight's performance. Take a look at yourselves at intermission. We're awfully glad you're here, and we hope you enjoy *All I Really Need to Know I Learned in Kindergarten.*"

The script for this preshow warm-up evolved out of a period of ad-libbing with the audience. Most of the jokes got good laughs, and served as a warm-up for the evening. You are welcome to adjust this preshow warm-up script to whatever works for you and your production. Please keep in mind that establishing a sense of comedy and friendliness is what this is all about.

APPENDIX F
Miscellaneous

PROPS/FURNITURE PLOT

1. Five oak schoolroom chairs, circa 1940 *(preset)*
2. One chalkboard *(preferably with black surface)*
   – free-standing on swivel yoke, oak *(preset)*
3. White chalk – large soft type found at art supply stores
   makes the most legible print from stage.
   Sidewalk chalk does not work. *(preset)*
4. Chalkboard erasers *(preset)*
5. Four letters 14 inches tall, to spell "LOOK" mounted on foam
   core placards 14"x18". One additional placard for
   exclamation point. *(The Kindergarten Song)*
6. Aluminum chaise lounge lawn chair – the kind with webbing
   and rivets. *(Larry Walters Flies)*
7. Stool – 30 inches high. *(Charles Boyer)*
8. Conductors podium – 24" square x 8" high, or chair can be
   substituted. *(Beethoven)*
9. Sink strainer *(Stuff in the Sink)*
10. Long tongs to hold sink strainer *(Stuff in the Sink)*
11. Helicopter seeds from a maple tree *(Donnie the Leaf Raker)*
12. Bench – made to look like three slabs of smooth, gray
    granite, 3' 6" long, 1' 4" wide, 1' 6" high. *(The Bench)*
13. White cloth bridal runner 30" wide *(MOTB)*
14. Rice *(MOTB)*
15. Crumpled letter, handwritten on notebook paper
    (Fathers and Sons)
16. A standard admissions form, mostly filled out *(Howard)*
17. 20" stool *(The Briefcase)*
18. Magazine *(Christmas/Valentine's Day)*

19. Round cafe table, 20"-24" diameter top x 28" high *(Geek Dancing)*
20. Blanket – comfortable, worn in, masculine
    (Tomb With a View)
21. Mirror ball *(Geek Dancing)*
22. Five small round mirrors *(plus extras for backup)*
    1 1/2" to 2 1/2" in diameter *(Are There Any Questions?)*
23. Slide of Charles Boyer

SOUND PLOT

CD of all sound effects can be ordered from Flat Five Press and Recording, 18 E. Main St., Salem, VA 24153, Phone: (540) 389-9427, E-mail: tom@flat5.com

A. Live cabled microphone at the piano for Pianist/Narrator.
B. Sound Cues
　　1. YES! OF COURSE I CAN! – School bell – 1950's/60's rapid report, electric clanger (4 seconds)

　　2. CINDERELLA – Thunderous applause and cheering (15 sec.)

　　3. HIDE AND SEEK – Children laughing and playing in leaves

　　4. LARRY WALTERS FLIES – Jet airliner sweeping by with a roar

　　5. BEETHOVEN –
　　　　a. Two telephone rings
　　　　b. Beethoven's Ninth – Final sequence of the Fourth Movement. *(See music in printed "Kindergarten" score for specifics.)*
　　　　c. Beethoven's Ninth. Ode to Joy, the biggest fullest vocal and orchestral section. *(See music in printed "Kindergarten" score for specifics.)* Note: Both Beethoven cues are very specific. Do not use any parts of the Ninth other than these two.

6. DONNIE THE LEAF RAKER –
    a. Two sets of six, loud, hard door knocks on wooden door.
       (Can also be done live from backstage over the mic.)
    b. One set of six knocks

7. PROBLEMS AND INCONVENIENCES – Cricket sounds late
    at night – six minutes, runs under entire story

8. PIGEONS – Thunder sound accompanying a cloudburst of rain

9. EXIT MUSIC – Orchestral of Edward Elgar's March #1.
    Pomp and Circumstance as in graduation recessional.
    Play from the beginning of the last loud chorus of the piece.

COSTUME PLOT

Each actor wears a base costume of contemporary street clothes.
A complete change for Act Two is desirable.

1. HIDE AND SEEK –
    3 colorful winter caps for kids. One can be a hood

2. BEETHOVEN –
    (BRANISLAV) can be performed in stocking feet,
    so appropriate socks are necessary

3. DONNIE THE LEAF RAKER –
    (KATHLEEN) fall sweater or jacket

4. THE STUFF IN THE SINK –
    (ED) backwards baseball cap, loud
    (JILL) loud pony tail accessory *(removable onstage)*
    (BRANISLAV) loud teen accessory, hat, vest, etc.

5. PROBLEMS AND INCONVENIENCES –
   (FRED) dark well-worn suit jacket, sweater-vest *(optional)*,
   wire-rim glasses
   (BRANISLAV) denim jacket, flannel overshirt, or CPO jacket

6. MOTB –
   (ED) navy blue blazer

7. FATHERS AND SONS –
   (BRANISLAV) casual Saturday knock-around jacket
   (circa 1958-1964)
   (ED) cardigan sweater
   (FRED) nylon jogging jacket – full zipper front
   (ALL) one baseball cap worn by all three men, really broken
   in. Favorite hat from college days, possibly with local major
   league logo

8. CHRISTMAS/VALENTINE'S DAY –
   (KATHLEEN, as 80-year-old woman) long red winter coat,
   older vintage. Square scarf folded into triangle, worn as
   head covering. Or hat
   Purse, snap-open top with easy access into it. Shoes, low,
   orthopedic-looking
   (FRED, as 86-year-old man) winter coat, older vintage
   Wool golf-style cap, or Homburg hat, scarf *(opt.)*
   (JILL) White lab coat

9. GEEK DANCING –
   (KATHLEEN) lovely dancing dress. Worn under coat in
   "Christmas/Valentine's Day."

The following is the text required for the scenic representation of the Kindergarten Creed, whether it be on the chalkboard, a banner, a pull-down screen or map-type scroll. It follows the lyric of the song, and not the original essay text from the book.

The Kindergarten Creed

Share.
Play Fair.
Don't hit People.
Don't take things that don't belong to you.
If you hurt someone, say you're sorry.
Clean up your own mess.
Wash your hands before you eat.
Hold hands and stick together when you cross the street.
Flush.
Live a balanced life.
Be aware of wonder.
LOOK.

(It is possible to fill in with lyrics from the song, but not from the original book.)

ROBERT FULGHUM Bio for Playbill and Publicity

Philosopher Robert Fulghum has published several best-selling books including: *All I Really Need to Know I Learned in Kindergarten, It was on Fire When I Lay Down on It, Uh-Oh, Maybe (Maybe Not), From Beginning to End, True Love* and *Words I Wish I Wrote*, setting records at the top of the *New York Times* bestseller list. There are currently more than 15 million copies of his books in print, published in 27 languages, in 93 countries.

Fulghum has performed in two television adaptations of his work for the Public Broadcasting System. He appeared twice with the Minneapolis Chamber Symphony, the first time conducting the last movement of Beethoven's Ninth. He has been a guest speaker at numerous colleges, conventions, and public events across the United States. The stage adaptation of his work (entitled *All I Really Need to Know I Learned in Kindergarten*) has been produced nationally in Chicago, Los Angeles, Washington, D.C., Seattle, Kansas City, Phoenix and Dallas, and other cities. Internationally, it has been produced in such cities as Manila, Singapore, Kuala Lumpur, and Prague.

Fulghum is committed to sharing his success and supports a variety of organizations, working in areas of literacy, education and human rights. His profits from *True Love* have gone to Habitat for Humanity, and those from *Words I Wish I Wrote* benefited Human Rights Watch.

An inveterate traveler, he's lived in Greece, France, Thailand and Japan, where he studied in a Zen Buddhist monastery. He has been deeply involved in the ecumenical work of The Orthodox Academy of Crete in Greece.

Fulghum was born in 1937 and grew up in Waco, Texas. In his youth he worked as a ditch digger, newspaper carrier, ranch hand, and singing cowboy, while riding the rodeo circuit on weekends. After college, and a short stint as an IBM salesman, he returned to graduate school to complete a degree in theology. For 22 years, he served as a parish minister of Unitarian churches in the Pacific Northwest. During this same period, he taught drawing, painting and philosophy at the Lakeside School in Seattle. Fulghum is also an accomplished painter and sculptor, and plays the guitar and mandocello.

He has four children and several grandchildren. He is very happily married to Lynn Edwards, a family physician, and lives on a houseboat in Seattle, Wash.

A NOTE FROM ROBERT FULGHUM (for inclusion in the playbill)

Sometime in 1985, a short essay most people call "That Thing About Kindergarten" won the International Refrigerator Award. It also won the Office Bulletin Board Sweepstakes, the Send-A-Copy-to-Your-Mom Trophy, and even the My-Rabbi-Read-It-In-His-Sermon Prize.

As I write now, "That Thing About Kindergarten" has traveled around the globe—translated into at least twenty-four languages.

And it became the title essay of the book *All I Really Need to Know I Learned in Kindergarten*, which has sold seven million copies in at least ninety-three countries.

The essay hangs in the halls of the U.S. Congress, on the walls of schools, and in prison cells. You can find it in high-tech scientific laboratories, your doctor's waiting room, and factory cafeterias.

The author of the kindergarten essay had his life turned topsy-turvy by it.

I know.

I am he.

Recently, to get some perspective on the whole hoo-ha, I stuck a copy of "Kindergarten" to the door of my own refrigerator (with four industrial magnets—none of those little cute ceramic deals for me—when I stick something to the fridge, it stays stuck). Anyhow ... I sat in my kitchen one night and stared at the lines that had altered my life and wondered: Why?

Why these words? Why me?

And most of all I wondered: Is it REALLY true that all I really need to know I learned in kindergarten?

On a quick critical read, the essay might easily be dismissed as a bit simple-minded, naive, cute, intellectually superficial.

The essay breaks the standard rule that important things are supposed to be hard to understand.

On the other hand, the essay asks the question asked sooner or later by every schoolchild staring out the window from a classroom desk and wondering: "Why am I here? Why do I have to go to school?"

We are sent to school to be civilized.

To be initiated into the most profound mysteries of society.

We are sent out of the home to meet the truth of the world.

Almost always the "world" turns out to be school. And no matter what that place of beginning in the world is called—day care, kindergarten, first grade—the experience is the same.

From the first, we are told in language we can understand, what has come to be prized as the foundation of community and culture. The teacher calls these first lessons "simple rules," but they are in fact the distillation of all the hard-won, field-tested fundamentals of civilization itself.

Not only are we told about these things, but we soon discover that we are in a lab course—we are going to be asked to live these precepts every day.

And they are not, it turns out, simple after all. No. *Elemental* is the word.

A carbon atom may be simply expressed in the symbol C, atomic number 6, but it is essential to the structure of life itself. Elemental. Not simple—with extremely complex implications.

I repeat. We are sent to school to be civilized.

And it is a bedrock value of civilization that knowledge is better than ignorance. We have found out the hard way. Experience and wisdom gained in the great march of humankind must be shared and passed on if the march is to continue.

What we learn in kindergarten will come up again and again in our lives as long as we live. In far more complex, polysyllabic forms, to be sure—lectures, encyclopedias, bibles, company rules, courts of law, sermons, and handbooks. We will be tested and examined over the years to see if we understand what we have learned.

Across the course of our lives we will wrestle with questions of right and wrong, good and bad, truth and lies. Again and again and yet again, we will come around to the place where we came in—to that room where the elemental notions about the human enterprise were handed to us with great care when we were very young—in kindergarten.

MEDIA QUOTES

"A refreshingly intimate combination of theatre and storytelling. Gentle...funny...joyous. Sparks of recognition ignited the audience."
The Chicago Sun Times

"Heartwarming, charming, funny and touching. The stories are about all of us."
National Public Radio

"Eighteen thought-provoking and sniffle-provoking vignettes left the audiences searching for hankies."
The Los Angeles Times

"Robert Fulghum's stories withstand the test of time. He is the Will Rogers or Mark Twain of our day."
Good Morning America

"A lighthearted, beautifully styled dramatization of Fulghum's writings."
Syracuse Herald Journal

"Here is a show for everyone. It produces laughter, smiles and tears as the audience sees themselves on stage."
Portsmouth Herald

"Fulghum's observations are as engaging as Spalding Gray's monologues, and as funny as the satire of a stand-up comedian."
The Chicago Daily Herald

"A gem of a show...The captivated audience nodded, smiled, cried, and nudged one another as they recognized familiar scenes that seem to have been taken out of their own lives."
The Philippine Star, Manila

Robert Fulghum's
ALL I REALLY NEED TO KNOW I LEARNED IN KINDERGARTENThirty-
Adapted by Ernest Zulia, Music and lyrics by David Caldwell

Thirty Minute Cuttings for High School Competitions

Dear Drama Teacher:

It is a pleasure to make the writings of Robert Fulghum available in script form for presentation by high school students. In addition to the full-length script for ALL I REALLY NEED TO KNOW I LEARNED IN KINDERGARTEN, we offer three options for thirty-minute cuttings designed for high school drama competions. Each cutting consists of six or seven stories and is designed to stand alone as a one-act play. These cuttings are not available in separate published form. It is necessary to work from the full-length script, using the guidelines below to reduce it to thirty minutes. Performance rights must be obtained from Dramatic Publishing.

Versions A and B feature only stories that in some way refer to kindergarten, children or childhood, as well as childrens' games, songs or sayings. These references serve as springboards to mature ideas and attitudes. The themes of childhood provide a strong unifying element. Version A requires some singing, Version B does not.

Version C features stories that have no references at all to childhood and kindergarten (with the exception of the opening piece, "Yes Of Course I Can"). This version opens and closes with stories set in a classroom, which provides the unifying element. Version C does not require singing. It is also possible to mix and match different stories in sequences other than those listed below.

Whichever version you choose, it is highly recommended that you incorporate the official piano underscoring and piano transitions. This greatly enhances the impact of the material, and helps the cutting flow. The piano score is avalable for rent through Dramatic Publishing. Specific piano cues and page numbers are noted below.

In many ways, ALL I REALLY NEED TO KNOW I LEARNED IN KINDERGARTEN is ideally suited to high school actors. It can incorporate any number of cast members, and can be done with as little scenery as one chair per actor. As a final suggestion, we strongly recommend referring to Appendices A and C in the back of the full script for tips on how to approach the material most effectively.

With over fifteen million books in print, the writings of Robert Fulghum have delighted readers around the world. And now, it is a joy to watch the stage adaptation reach a whole new audience. We wish you all the best with your encounter with *KINDERGARTEN.*

Warm regards,

Ernest Zulia, and David Caldwell

Robert Fulghum's
ALL I REALLY NEED TO KNOW I LEARNED IN KINDERGARTEN
Thirty-Minute Cuttings for High School Competitions

Version A (Tied together with kindergarten and childhood themes. Some singing required)

Yes! Of Course I Can
    (music cue: 1. Opening, pp.1-2 in the score)
Kindergarten Song
    (2. music: The Kindergarten Song, pp. 3-19)
Spider
    (music cue: Spider, pp. 219-224)
Solomon Islands (or Hide and Seek)
    (music cue: Solomon Islands, p. 201 [or 4. Hide And Seek, pp. 21-
    22])
Howard
    (music cue: 19. After Howard, p. 120)
Cinderella
    (3. Cinderella music Cues, p. 20; after m. 6, cut to #24, Curtain
    Call, pp.   152-154)

Version B (Tied together with kindergarten and childhood themes. No singing required)

Yes! Of Course I Can
    (music cues: 1. Opening, pp. 1-2; 2. The Kindergarten Song [play
    mm. 1-8 softly under the lines "What went wrong...of course I
    can?"])
Cinderella
    (3. music cues: Cinderella Cues and After Cinderella, p. 20)
Hide And Seek
    (4. music cues: Hide And Seek, pp. 21-22)
Spider
    (music cue: Spider, pp. 219-224)
Solomon Islands
    (music cue: Solomon Islands, p. 201)

(Version B continued)
Howard
        (19. Music cue: After Howard, p. 120)
Stuff In The Sink (Spoken Version)
        (Music cue: After Donnie/The Stuff In The Sink, pp. 202-205
        [start with the pickup to m. 6]; 24. Curtain Call, pp. 152-154)
(If cutting runs too long, eliminate Solomon Islands or Howard,
maintaining the same running order.)

Version C

Yes! Of Course I Can
        (music cues: 1. Opening, pp. 1-2; 2. The Kindergarten Song [play
        mm. 1-8 softly under the lines "What went wrong...of course I
        can?"])
Larry Walters Flies
        (5. Music cue: Larry Walters Flies, pp. 23-24)
MOTB (Ensemble version found on page 155)
        (14. Music cues: MOTB, pp. 92-96)
Problems And Inconveniences (or Beethoven, or Fathers And Sons.
    or Christmas/Valentine's Day)
        (10. Music cue: After Problems And Inconveniences, p. 62)
Are There Any Questions?
        (23. Music cue: pp. 143-145 [play through m. 43];
         24. Curtain   Call, pp. 152-154)

WHAT PEOPLE ARE SAYING about *All I Really Need to Know I Learned in Kindergarten...*

"Wonderful! We could tell how close to home the stories were from the look in the eyes of our audience." *[Mr. or Ms.] Exler,*
Seckman Senior High School., Imperial, Mont.

"What a joy to produce! Not only did the students perform it, they GREW by working on it as well." *Mr. J.D. Gonzalez,*
Kellogsville High School, Grand Rapids, Mich.

"...I particularly enjoy the rhythm of the play itself, the beautiful language of each character. Although separate, each passage is interconnected in some way, making the audience able to identify with the entire piece." *Richard Marcucci, Moorestown Friends School, Moorestown, N.J.*

"Kindergarten is disarmingly moving. It builds to a strong climax which we didn't see coming. The audience was shaken and stirred—but enormously surprised!" *Marianne Casey/Marvin Budd,*
Little Theatre of Greeneville, Greeneville, Tenn.

"A warm, witty, touching show—enthusiastically acted by students and well received by an appreciative audience. We could all identify with these 'slices of life.' " *Sandra Camphor,*
Ocean Springs High School, Ocean Springs, Miss.

"It was the most satisfying play I've ever directed. (I've directed over 50 plays.) This is the best possible choice for a high school play I could recommend—it is warm, funny, poignant, as well as thought-provoking. Both my students and the adult audience love it!" *Judy Edwards,*
Vacaville High School, Vacaville, Calif.

"This was one of our most successful productions. It called for the best from the actors and gave them a chance to explore many characters and moods. It was a great challenge and fun to meet." *James Moody,*
Northside High School, Fort Smith, Ark.

"Great show! Easy to use for flexible casting. The script makes it easy to adapt for H.S. use! " *Joe D. King,*
North Central High School, Indianapolis, Ind.